CROSS-COUNTRY SKIING

by
Ned Gillette and John Dostal

SECOND EDITION

The Mountaineers • Seattle

THE MOUNTAINEERS: Organized 1906 "... to explore, study, preserve and enjoy the natural beauty of the Northwest."

Copyright 1983 by Edward F. Gillette and John Dostal. All rights reserved.

Published by The Mountaineers, 715 Pike Street, Seattle, Washington 98101

Published simultaneously in Canada by Douglas & McIntyre, Ltd., 1615 Venables Street, Vancouver, B.C. V5L 2H1

Manufactured in the United States of America
First edition, first printing October 1979, second printing December 1979, third printing January 1981, fourth printing October 1982
Second edition 1983

Edited by Diane Hammond, designed by Marge Mueller

Cover photo: Lisa Paschall and Jim Speck at Galena Ski Touring area, Sun Valley

Library of Congress Cataloging in Publication Data

Gillette, Ned, 1945-
    Cross-country skiing.

    Includes index.
    1. Cross-country skiing.   I. Dostal, John.
II. Title.
GV855.3.G54   1983   796.93   83-13319
ISBN 0-89886-079-2

Contents

Start of the American Birkebeiner, Cable, Wisconsin

Preface

Except for the Olympics or World Championships, the Holmenkollen in Oslo, Norway, is the most prestigious ski competition on the year's calendar. Fifty thousand spectators arrange themselves to shout frenzied encouragement along the fifty-kilometer cross-country race course. To win is to reach the top of international racing. To participate was a dream realized for Ned Gillette on his first trip to Europe. At the sixth feeding station, manned by then U.S. team coach John Caldwell, the track was downhill just enough to keep Ned gliding. Skiing through a corridor of vocal Norwegians who surely discerned that his inexperienced body was beginning to burn out, he eagerly took the cup of energy-laden liquid from John's extended hand. With a sweeping motion worthy of a champion beer chugger, he reared back, the better to throw the drink directly down. Too far! One ski was launched into the air, sweeping above his head as he, like a drunk slowly crumbling, landed neatly on his rear in front of his first international audience.

Since that flamboyant buttocks arrest in 1968, Ned has tried the strict business world, but skis seemed to appear under his desk. He directed ski schools in California, Colorado, and Vermont; then pioneered adventure skiing expeditions in the Arctic, China, and the Himalaya. Skiing became serious enjoyment.

But it was the recurring memory of the Holmenkollen crumple—humorous in retrospect but devastating to young pride at the time—that caused him to consider adding another book on cross-country skiing to those already on the shelves. Why another one? It seemed to him that other books assume you'll take the nourishment they offer in one neat gulp. His experience teaching, racing, and adventuring suggests that it often goes over the shoulder or down the chest, or that occasionally, like he was, the skier is airborne in the process. He has yet to find a book fully realizing that, as his colleague John Dostal says, "When you take technique off the page and onto the snow, it can be a pretty messy process."

Cross-country is more than skiing on the flat.

Along with descriptions and demonstrations of competent skiing, you'll find in the pages that follow as much on what can go wrong and what to do about it as what is right, and some exercises and suggestions on how to get a feel for the maneuvers—in short, not just ideal execution but what you'll really need to know to be comfortable on your skis and clever on the trail, whether it is a touring-center track, an alpine slope, a marathon race course, or a backcountry trek.

As at Holmenkollen, another offer of energy-laden aid was eagerly accepted, this time more successfully...this time from John Dostal. Thus did the writing of this book become a happy collaboration between one trained in skiing who took to writing and one trained in writing who took to skiing, a collaboration that came out of the teaching of skiing, by two who have been directors of one of the country's largest ski touring centers and ski schools.

Our first edition was written four years ago. Why a new one? Foremost, cross-country skiing has continued to evolve. Skiers have attacked dramatic terrain with cross-country gear. The telemark uprising has turned into a revolution. Refined techniques and the marathon skate are cutting racing times. The kind of skis once reserved in racing rooms for elite competitors now fill retail racks. Skis that had metal edges were redesigned for the demands of steeper skiing. New waxes have been brewed with abandon. Waxless skis perform better than ever.

As the sport has grown, various new books have appeared, each covering a single aspect of it. We continue to keep cross-country between two covers because we believe that those who enjoy cross-country most are complete skiers, not tied to the tracks nor bound to the backcountry, but ready for either depending on the progress of a winter's conditions. Furthermore, techniques are interrelated: the way your knee lines up over your foot for maximum glide when you're riding a racing ski in a fast track is the way your knee lines up over your foot for grip while making a steep traverse on climbing skins in the backcountry. The same skate that takes you across the field in the mass start of a marathon takes you across high mountain plateaus with a backpack on spring corn snow.

Much of this book is about technique, because there is technique in the sport, despite what some people say. The discussion emphasizes real situations and practical advice rather than theory and prescription. Drawing on our teaching and skiing experience, we also show a variety of skiers in a variety of snows and terrain—all to the end of supple skiing.

Introduction

Origins and Echoes

When Ned Gillette and Jan Reynolds were in Manchuria teaching skiing to Chinese youngsters still happily using handcarved wooden skis, and having never seen wax, it was evident how far skiing had come in North America. This real-life skiing museum brought back thoughts on the origins of skiing.

A Stone Age carving discovered in a Norwegian cave north of the Arctic Circle shows a stick figure riding long skis in the pursuit of elk. Date: 2,000 B.C. Written reference to *skridfinnar* (sliding Finns) was made by Procopius (526-559 A.D.). Norsemen used skis in early times to travel, hunt and fight. Often skis were of unequal length: a short one with fur fixed to the bottom for grip, and a long one on the other foot for glide. Balancing with a single pole, a skier could scooter over the rolling terrain of the Scandinavian countries. (Alpine skiing later was developed in the Alps, enabling local people to negotiate the steep mountainous slopes of Central Europe.)

As early as 1200 A.D., during the Battle of Oslo, King Sverre of Norway sent ski-equipped scouts on extensive reconnaissance missions. The scouts were called birchlegs because of their custom of wrapping their legs in bark to protect against cold.

As the hardships of life in northern climates eased, skiing evolved away from strict utilitarian purposes toward sport. In 1779 a Danish priest, Father Nicolay Jonge, mentioned that, "In Norway, it is common for kids to practice skiing so extensively that even along the coast of Norway, where there is no practical need for them, skis are used for fun." Skiing was on the way to being the national sport of Norway.

The flowering of skiing as a sport was given impetus by two remarkable Norwegians who broke with tradition. The first was Sondre Norheim, the best skier in the Telemark district. He and his country boys dominated ski competitions in Christiania (now Oslo) starting in 1868. How? By

Kahiltna Glacier, Mt. McKinley.

Equipment has changed a lot since these skis.

superior technique bolstered by innovative equipment, which gave a whole new appearance to the young sport.

Norheim hit upon the idea of a binding that much improved steering control. In addition to the old toe strap, he used twisted birch roots around his heel to give a rigid, binding connection to the ski. This was the first modern binding. It gave him the ability to do precise turns of linked beauty. Going further with his improvements, he moved another step closer to modern skiing by building the first pair of skis with side cut. Light enough to bend during the force of a turn, the maneuverable skis allowed real carved turns.

On the slopes, Norheim developed the telemark turn, which further eliminated skidding during turns. With his controlled, elegant S-turns he outskied all contestants at the Christiania meets, even at forty-two years of age. Newspapers trumpeted, "Sondre Norheim could come down like lightning and suddenly stop in a second . . . . a new era has arisen in skiing."

This new era was dramatized by Fridtjof Nansen's celebrated crossing of Greenland in 1888. It was a bold, pioneering step, pointing out the dependable use of skis in conquering the most inhospitable regions of the earth. The expedition took forty days. On skis, Nansen's team dragged sledges over the height of the icecap and covered five hundred kilometers.

In 1911 another Norwegian explorer, Roald Amundsen, skied to the South Pole. His relatively easy trek emphasized the tremendous advantages of gliding over snow. In tragic contrast was the fate suffered by Robert Falcon Scott, victim of a skiless tradition: his team bogged down, exhausted from hauling sledges on foot.

Closer to home, Norwegian immigrants brought skiing to North America in the mid-1800s. The most famous of these Americanized Norsemen was Snowshoe Thompson, originally from the Telemark district. During the 1850s Snowshoe carried mail over the crest of California's Sierra Nevada for the hefty fee of two dollars per letter. As communication grew, so did his loads, often nearing one hundred pounds. The ninety-mile trip took three days to the east, but only two days on the return due to long downhill slopes.

He was not the only "plankhopper." Fierce ski competitions erupted throughout the gold camps of the Sierra, and big money was wagered on rocketing schusses. It is said that one daredevil plummeted downhill at eighty-eight miles an hour. Cross-country skiing as utilitarian travel and exhilarating sport was here to stay.

Untracked snow is a joy.

⟨*1*⟩

Getting Started

We've heard many observers of cross-country (particularly those of an alpine persuasion) say that it is a monotonous, dull, plodding sport. If you do ski walking only, it may be. But once you get the feeling of momentum carrying you down the trail, of being up and over your skis, of gentle and secure forward speed, it is a totally new sport with a subtle, gravity-defying fluidity: the more speed, the greater sense of release — even true on uphills where, with a little extra effort, you can scamper rather than plod.

To get that feeling, it's important to secure a good environment for learning. If you attempt to learn in unbroken snow, you'll have a hard time getting into a smooth glide. And icy, rutted snow demands a degree of control of your skis that you need time to develop. Skills learned on trails can be transferred to off-trail conditions; going the other way is harder. Learning under the right conditions means that speed becomes less scary, that as you progress, everything seems to slow down. You seem to have more time to make turns. Instead of merely hanging on, hoping to get through a difficult section without crashing, you are looking ahead and anticipating how you can maintain and possibly increase your speed. You begin to feel more powerful, more in control — you are skiing the trail rather than the trail skiing you.

Whether you're learning from a book or an instructor, don't create mental obstacles that will get in the way of surmounting the physical ones. Occasionally students introduce themselves to their instructors by announcing, "I want you to know that you're dealing with a klutz." For these people and for the instructor there is heavy psychological weather ahead. It is not very helpful at the beginning of a lesson to get down on yourself. This will only short-circuit your progress. So will competing with other students or your instructor, or assuming that you can learn all of cross-country skiing in a day, or concentrating on your failures and forgetting your successes.

A successful businessman from New York, outfitted with the latest racing gear, expected to become an expert skier in a week of intensive instruction. His expectations so greatly exceeded what was possible in the time he had given himself that he became unwittingly unreceptive to learning and made little progress—leading to an acute case of frustration. His problem was compounded by a sense of being always on display. When we were out skiing together, as soon as another instructor approached he promptly fell off his skis, probably thinking, "There's another one who is going to see how poorly I ski!" The second instructor had no idea that he had been called for jury duty. To help our student understand the bind he had put himself in, we asked if he could make us shrewd and successful investment bankers in the same time period.

For many skiers the words "falling" and "failing" not only sound alike but equal each other. As soon as backside touches snow, the self-indictment begins. Much better to remember that snow is nontoxic, and try to focus on *why* you fell: look at the track your ski made, remember where you were looking or where your hands were. Students who have fallen on downhills will often be asked by an instructor, "Where were your hands?" Often a quick, protective, "In the wrong place," is the response. But what the instructor is after is physical focusing, not psychological judgment. The skier who is relaxed enough to say, "It felt as if they got behind me," is making an important discovery about skiing. If good skiers were to get down on themselves every time they took a wind-milling half-gainer at high speeds, they'd be too depressed to wax their skis for another day's run!

Another day's run (call it insightful repetition) is just what is needed. You don't have to be in a class to tune up your skiing. You just have to be willing to go back over the section of trail that threw you, practicing and changing your approach until you have mastered it. "You make it look so easy. I feel sort of unbalanced being on one ski at a time," says the despairing student to the instructor, who

For better skiing match your instructor stride-for-stride.

may ski daily and take an off-season vacation on skis. "And why not?" replies the instructor. "You've been on skis for all of ten minutes." Remember the first time you drove an automobile? Was your timing a bit shaky in traffic? So too in learning to ski: there is simply no substitute for getting kilometers under your skis. And you have to prevent your expectations from boiling over while you're accumulating the distance, perfecting your technique so you feel comfortable on your boards in all trail conditions and instinctively do things right. How do you eat an elephant? One bite at a time.

Progress is relative. Getting a little jogging glide on the flats may provide the beginning or casual skier with all the speed desired, while the marathon foot runner aspiring to equal past road-running times will be striving for much more, as will the alpine racer who tries to carve high-speed turns on skinny skis and the hard-core backpacker who wants to trek through the wilderness in winter. Levels of expertise must be measured by your own standards. What is possible for one skier may not be for another, and expectations that are now beyond reach only lead to frustration. Not being able to do a parallel turn doesn't mean you cannot have fun on cross-country skis. Also, it's remarkable how agile and coordinated everyone is in some aspect of skiing. One woman was distressed that she couldn't learn to snowplow as fast as others in her class. She had to be reminded that, if she wanted to keep score, she was at the head of the class in skiing uphill.

It is useful occasionally to take things apart and monitor your skills as you ski. Think of it as a checklist or tune-up. Take things one at a time, focusing on hands, body position, leg movement, and so forth.

Skiing Ellesmere Island.

Free and Easy on the Flat

The diagonal stride is really cross-country skiing's emblem: a skier stretched out on the flat, gliding in easy alliance with gravity. We've long heard the sport promoted with the slogan "if you can walk, you can ski." Walking *is* where it begins, with first timers usually standing straight up and hesitantly advancing one ski and foot, getting used to the tippy novelty.

Some skiers stay resolutely upright, never getting beyond a ponderous shuffle, never getting that glide. How to

More gorilla for more glide.

get it? Change your posture. Slump to begin to stride. In short, more gorilla for more glide.

The biomechanics are inescapable: hunch over, round your back, and you'll turn walking into gliding. Moreover, you will feel more secure and less wobbly on your skis.

Now begin to jog on your skis. It's like springing across a stream. Commit your whole body to the forward effort, and you land not on the jogger's asphalt road but a platform sliding on the snow. Stay hunched over and that platform won't slide out from under you.

We've left you balancing on one foot gliding along. How do you obtain a grip in this slippery stuff to continue jogging? A rubber sole is secure on asphalt in the summer, but what about these skis?

Listen to a seven-year-old explaining things to an obvious first timer: "See, all you have to do is put a little pressure on your skis as you go forward." Here in one short sentence of simplicity and sophistication is the essence of diagonal striding.

At first get a feeling for short jogging strides and leaning forward on your skis.

This pressure is called kick. When your weight is on the forward, gliding ski, press (kick) down on it so it will grip the snow, providing a platform from which to launch yourself onto the other ski, which is coming forward—a skier's form of jogging. Many beginners think that what makes you move forward is only a "scootering" or pushing back with one ski, but you need to press down for grip first. Think of how you would jog on a slippery, snow-covered road, pressing down when your weight is directly over your forward or kicking foot for maximum traction.

Now try to put it all together, jogging with a steady rhythm. Avoid any distinct hesitation at the end of each stride. You don't "freeze" at the end of each stride as you run down the street, do you? A good way to feel this rhythm is to follow a good skier who is skiing slowly, matching strides. Or try jogging up a moderate hill as if you didn't have skis on. This will speed up your rhythm to a point where you can't think every segment of your stride through to complicated disaster and will give you security if you're worried about catapulting over the tips of your skis.

Learn the rhythm of cross-country without poles.

With practice you'll be able to lengthen your stride and increase your speed.

No-Pole Work

To improve rhythm and balance, try skiing without poles, letting your hands pull you out over your skis and down the track. You'll have one less piece of equipment to think about. Allow your arms to swing back and forth comfortably to set your tempo, keeping your hands relatively low in front. If you can see them up in front of your face, they're too high and will throw you back off your forward ski instead of pulling you onto it.

Although you see experienced skiers swooping down the track with long strides, stick to a short jogging stride which will make steady rhythm easier to maintain. Long strides lead to bad habits in the beginning, the most prominent of which is setting your weight too far back so that your hips are behind rather than over your front foot and ski. After all, you don't jog with a ten-foot stride, do you? Many beginners notice the tail of an experienced skier's rear ski lifting high off the snow, and try to copy it. This is simply the follow-through from leaning forward over a kick which is powerful, just as you'd follow through in a sweeping arc after hitting a tennis ball. In time this long stride and leg follow-through will develop naturally. Forcing it at the beginning could disrupt your rhythm.

Weight

One of the best ways to feel a definite weight shift from one ski to the other is to skate on your skis. You'll be forced to throw your weight from ski to ski as you push off like a speed skater. This will already be familiar to alpine skiers, who will find it easier on cross-country equipment and may be able to add a familiar double-pole push. Select a flat or ever-so-slight downhill packed area. Start by striding forward in your ordinary diagonal stride. Once you are moving, let your ski tips splay out in a V. Edge your skis to the inside (that is, roll your ankles to put your weight on the inside edges) and push off one, then the other, with a constant rhythm.

Weight shift is accomplished by loosening your hips. To loosen hips and stretch out your stride, bend your knees or lower your stance a little as if you were receiving a tennis serve. Many track skiers, even those with years of experience, diagonal-stride with blocked or stiff hips, caused by straight or stiff knees. The hips don't come forward with the gliding or forward ski or go back with the kicking leg. The result is reduced extension in the stride, little power in the kick, little uphill grip, little momentum, and only slight weight shift onto the gliding ski.

Skating gives you a feeling for rhythm and weight shift.

(Top) WRONG! Stiff knees block hips and prevent weight shift.
(Below) RIGHT! Lower your stance to loosen up and stretch.

To prove to yourself how stiff knees block your entire technique, try to ski with locked knees and feel what it does to your movements. If you still cannot loosen your hips, think of "poling through your hip" with each stride. As your arm pushes back, your hip comes forward.

Another way to get the feeling of weight shift is by jogging up a gradual hill on skis. Decreased speed and increased tempo allow you to bounce more completely onto the forward ski.

Poling

Improve your kick and glide by working on your arms? Absolutely. Correct arm and poling motion is the key to better skiing. The way you use your poles dictates your rhythm, body position, relaxation, and speed.

Many beginners use their poles solely as outriggers or as canes for balance. Outriggers help you stay upright but supply no push down the track. Abandon the notion of poles as training wheels. You should be working your arms vigorously, depending on the grip of your wax and the incline of the trail, to supply a good deal of your forward power.

Plant your pole (stick it into the snow) in front so it is angled backward for immediate push. Push straight down and back past your hip. Your poling motion should take place half in front and half in back of your body when skiing on the flat, or you lose much of your pushing potential.

To recover the pole, bring it forward at an angle, swinging your hand like a pendulum past your hip. Don't try to lift the pole vertically over the snow. This can lead to some pretty bizarre recovery motions, including the Swim, the Windmill, the Roundhouse, the Disposal of the Dead Mouse, and the Pattycake, all of which we've seen in teaching over the years. One thing they all have in common is lifting rather than swinging the pole forward. And that means loss of momentum and an upright rather than a forward body position.

Be definite both in planting and recovering the pole. A weak action or a super-slow rhythm will allow your pole to skip along the snow as it is coming forward and throw you off balance and timing.

Use your poles for setting rhythm and pushing yourself forward.

If pushing the poles past your hip seems awkward, you may be gripping them too tightly. Cradle the pole in your hand. Relax your fingers. For maximum thrust with a relaxed arm, release your grip on the handle as you extend back. Some skiers let go of the pole completely, allowing it to hang from the strap. As an arm swings forward, the snug strap pulls the pole back into the hand. Others prefer to release the pole only with the last three fingers, which gives total extension, yet allows control of the pole action with thumb and forefinger.

If your pole inexplicably seems to flap out of your grip, it may be because the handle lacks a knob at the top which fits between thumb and forefinger. If this is the case, you can make one by taping the top inch of the strap to the handle with several turns of electricians' tape.

For more power and efficiency, your arms should swing like pendulums from the shoulders when poling, as they do when you walk. Larger shoulder and back muscles provide more thrust than arm muscles. Shoulders that are locked force the arms to move only from the elbows, resulting in weak, choppy poling. Comfortably bent arms provide maximum power for the energy expended. Think of how you would hammer a nail. Would you hammer with arms straight or slightly bent?

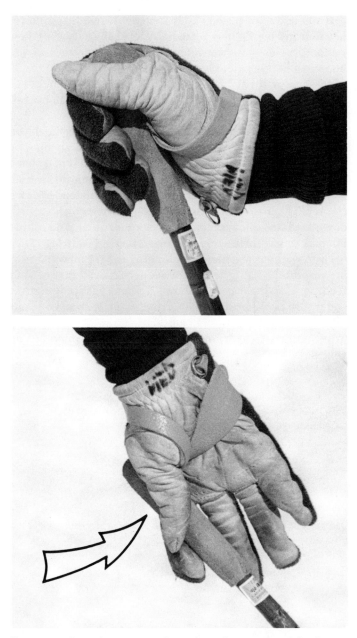

For easy poling release your grip on the pole as you push back.

If you're a slow-paced skier, you should keep your hands low in front: bring them up to belly level but no higher. Low hands provide maximum thrust at slow speeds. As you become a better skier carrying real speed down the track, your arms will lift higher, and you'll have a tremendous sensation of the swing of your arms setting your overall pace. Your whole body is drawn ahead by your arms coming through quickly. It's just like running: recall how much you work your arms when you want to move into a sprint.

Hands lifted too high in front bring your upper body back off your skis with each stride in a bobbing motion which directs much of your energy up into the air instead of down the trail. It also slows your tempo, provides only a push down into the snow instead of a push forward, and allows no push or extension of your poling behind your leg.

Even worse is the habit of reaching too far forward with an absolutely straight arm. This poisons the rest of your technique, as it slows your tempo, lessens your power, gives you a sore back, prevents you from being forward on your gliding ski, stiffens your knees, fouls up your rhythm, and gives you a late kick, making you generally impotent on your skis.

WRONG! Incorrect use of the arms fouls up the rest of your technique.

Without using your legs you cannot afford to be inefficient in your poling.

Try this exercise to get the feel of efficient poling. Find a slightly downhill track and push yourself along with your poles alone, in an alternating rhythm. Don't use your legs, but make sure you bend your knees slightly—it's easier. Working hard? That's how much energy you should use, even when striding. Experiment to discover what is most efficient. Straighten your arms, bend them, angle your poles differently, raise your hands high or low in front, grip your poles differently. You'll soon discover the most efficient means of propelling yourself. It doesn't take bulging muscles for this one, only correct technique. Once you feel it, you'll ski a new and easier way.

Double Poling

One skiing maneuver uses arms only: double poling, in which you use both poles together to push yourself along, thus giving your legs a rest. Use it whenever you want to keep up speed on fast flats or on gradual downhills. Beyond this, get a feeling for when double poling works best by skiing with someone else. If the other person is striding, try double poling and see if it's more efficient. Double poling is also extremely stable because you are standing securely on both skis, which makes the technique useful where the trail is broken, chaotic, or icy. Touring skiers, we've found, don't double-pole as much as they should.

When a group (including Ned Gillette) skied across Alaska's Brooks Range in 1972, they came across a huge area of overflow ice. The Koyukuk River had frozen all the way to the bottom, damming itself and creating an ice-skating rink measuring two miles by three miles. The party had no alternative but to ski over the ice as they entered the "Gates of the Arctic." They had no metal edges on their skis. Solution? Double poling for three miles. It

To double-pole "fall" forward onto your poles, then push with your arms.

was the most stable technique they could use, since they'd forgotten their ice skates!

Double poling may look as if it is done totally with your arms, but most of the power is generated by the weight of your upper body compressing downward and pushing back on the ski poles. Your upper body "falling onto your poles" gives you a free ride with little muscle work.

Start by reaching forward with arms slightly bent at the elbows and planting your poles pointed slightly back. Bend at the waist, dropping forward and down on your poles. It is critical to keep your arms in a fixed position, the angle of your elbow unchanged, as you compress in order to transfer your upper-body power to your poles. Letting your arms give way is inefficient. Only when you're bent over (with your upper body nearly parallel to the snow if you're a power skier) should you complete the double pole by straightening your arms with a final push.

Double poling is the only time in cross-country skiing that you hinge at the waist, up and down. Pretend you are pumping an old-fashioned railroad handcar up and down as you move along the trail. The downward compression of

WRONG! Don't "sit in a chair."

Adding a kick to your double pole will provide more push at slower speeds.

the body onto the poles is done at the waist, not the knees. Your knees should be relaxed and flexed a bit but should not provide the dropping motion. This causes the most common error of double poling ("sitting in a chair"), which puts your weight back, absorbing the force that should propel you down the track.

When double poling becomes too hard or slows you down, add a kick to your rhythm before you revert to your slower-speed diagonal stride.

Slippery Strides

If you are slipping and not getting your skis to grip the snow, it can be for one of several reasons:

• Wrong or insufficient wax or ineffective waxless pattern.

• Too stiffly cambered skis for your technique or the snow conditions. Try a softer pair, waxed the same.

• No weight shift onto your front ski.

• Pushing only backward when you kick — what technicians call a late kick. Get an earlier and more powerful kick by starting to put pressure on your skis with your toes; imagine your boots are cleated and that you're trying to get those cleats dug right into the snow.

Herringboning is a useful technique for narrow gullies.

Uphill

For most alpine skiers there is nothing sublime about climbing a hill (they've invented other means of dealing with vertical). Even cross-country skiers may find uphills tedious and troublesome. But covering great gulps of terrain, uphill or down, is one of the pleasures of touring. With proper technique and equipment, skiing uphill can be an easy and graceful pleasure, more cruising than hiking.

You need make only a few adjustments to your flat-track technique and have a willingness to raise your pulse rate a little to ski straight up most hills. Get a feeling of where your weight is on your skis. Lean too far forward and your skis will slip because your center of gravity is in front of your feet; lean too far back and you will feel slow and awkward, as if you are sitting in a chair and pulling yourself up the slope.

Try to be light on your feet and to feel the snow under your skis. Shorten your stride, just as you would if you were running the hill on foot without skis. Jog up the hills as if you didn't have skis on—it's the thing you know best.

Arms usually supply lots of the power on the uphills, especially if your skis are waxed a bit too slippery. Keep your hands fairly low and your poles angled back so you can push effectively. All your energy should be going forward up the hill. Many people bounce up and down, half their energy wasted into the air. And they may even pick their skis off the ground rather than sliding them forward. Keep your head steady and your arms moving straight ahead, and your body will follow.

These techniques will work for you regardless of the speed you choose to attack the hills. Many beginners have to develop not only the technique but the strength to ski uphill. They mix in some ski walking with their ski jogging. Or they should. Plodding up every hill won't yield results, but slowing down and walking when you have to — as long as you pay attention to technique — will. Don't straighten up and step, but slide your ski forward, feeling your weight come onto it. When the angle of the hill lessens, or when you catch your breath, get your arms moving and start skiing again.

You will get a good grip on the snow if your weight is over your kicking foot. As your foot comes forward, "hit" the ski with your heel for just an instant. This is the easiest way to achieve correct weight position: if your heel can contact the ski, your weight must be directly over that foot. Then roll over the ball of your foot as you kick back and propel yourself forward.

Hills don't have to be difficult if you keep your weight over your feet and jog lightly up.

WRONG! Don't make it hard on yourself.

Here is the classic predicament that many people work themselves into on a hill, guaranteeing a slip.

1. Poles are straight up and down, supplying no power.

2. Knees are straight so the heel cannot contact the ski for proper weight placement.

3. Body is way bent over at the waist, putting the body's center of gravity far ahead of the feet. Simply looking up the hill will help put your weight properly on your skis. (For years native Vermonters have used the term "way bent over" to describe an extraordinarily stupid person.)

Herringboning

When the hill becomes very steep or your wax starts to slip, it's time to break into a duck walk for extra grip.

Spread the tips of your skis far apart, keeping the tails together to form a wedge, or reverse snowplow. Tip your skis severely on their inside edges so they bite into the snow for hold. Bend your knees forward and inside. Step *forward* in this spread-eagle position in your regular ski-striding rhythm. Chop little steps in the snow with each stride. If the herringbone feels awkward, you are probably waddling uphill with your weight too far back or stepping on the tail of the opposite ski.

Try to get up the hill with as narrow a herringbone as possible. Maybe you need to spread your tips only two feet apart and use your edges to get up; no need to automatically spread them an extra couple of feet, making it more awkward.

Sidestepping

On steeper inclines where you are hesitant about negotiating the terrain, sidestepping is the technique of last resort. It's slow and tedious, but wonderfully secure going both up and down.

Place your skis across the fall line and roll your ankles into the slope to edge your skis for grip. (The fall line is defined as a snowball's path of least resistance down the hill.) Step up or down by shifting your weight from one ski to the other. In deep snow, control your ski by lifting up with your toes and pressing down with your heel. On an icy slope, lean your body away from the slope for secure edge bite. Leaning into the hill will push your edges off the snow, often leading to a bruising slide.

You can get a good feeling for this maneuver while still on the flat. Stand on your skis, extend one arm to the side, and have a friend tug steadily, trying to pull you off balance. You'll put up maximum resistance by driving your knees away from the pull. Look down and notice that your upper body is over your feet and that your skis are automatically on their edges. This may feel scary on a steep slope as you are poised looking down a breathtaking pitch, but your driving knees and edged skis will give you a reassuring platform.

When you start slipping, break into a herringbone for more climbing power.

Traversing and Tacking

Instead of sidestepping straight up or down, traversing, or zigzagging, on a gradual angle is often an easier solution to a steep slope, especially when toting a heavy backpack. A clever route tacking around the worst obstacles is extremely efficient in deep snow or on long mountain tours where energy must be conserved.

Tacking is a slightly higher-speed version of a traverse, combining straight uphill skiing, a slight herringbone, and plenty of edging. Diagonal-stride uphill at the steepest angle you can manage that will still allow you to move quickly. Change directions by taking an uphill step off to the other side. Less tedious than the herringbone, tacking can be fast and subtle.

Kick Turning

How do you turn around at the end of each zig or zag? A kick turn will change your direction one hundred and

Although it may look like it, you don't have to be a ballet dancer to change directions.

eighty degrees. The quicker you do this little ballet maneuver, the better your chances are of success.

Kick your lower ski forward, then around in an arc so it faces the opposite direction. You are now standing like Charlie Chaplin, feet pointing in opposite directions. You're in fourth position ballet. Forget the plié. To hesitate is to lose. Quickly shift weight onto the ski pointed in the new direction and bring the other one around parallel. Try this one on the flat the first few times, working up to steeper terrain. When skiers have trouble with kick turns it's usually because they swivel the ski out to the side to turn it. No matter what length of ski you're on, it's still too long to turn it that way. The better way is to lift your toe and the tip of the ski straight up (you'll feel it in your shin), then flop the ski over.

On steep slopes, some skiers prefer to kick-turn facing downhill, as it's easier to get the skis free of the hill. Others prefer to turn into the hill, reckoning that if they lose it at midpoint, they'll be closer to a self-arrest position.

Downhill skiing adds to the pleasure of cross-country.

Downhill

Many skiers without downhill experience are surprised at the amount of downhill they have to deal with on cross-country skis. Some feel there is a conspiracy between gravity and a well-waxed ski: point the skis downhill and they seem to have a will of their own. But downhill skiing on cross-country skis for both experienced skiers and novices has recently been getting the attention it deserves. First, speeding securely down hills is rather addictive and a real tonic for skiers whose local touring trails are getting too familiar. Second, for beginning cross-country skiers, the downhill sections, not the flats, are the real enemy to overcome on the way to overall enjoyment of the sport.

Downhill skiers are adding cross-country to their winter pleasures and cross-country skiers are riding the lifts with loose heels and heading for steep backcountry terrain on light equipment. Many slopes traditionally skied with heavy ski-mountaineering equipment are now being skied with three-pin equipment. Cross-country downhill on metal-edged skis has even become a sport unto itself, a new challenge, a new use of nordic gear. It is three times the fun of alpine skiing at half the speed.

All over the country skiers seem to be rediscovering the early days of alpine skiing of the 1930s. Cross-country skiers in the town we live in often head to the top of Mount Mansfield, Vermont's highest peak, to ski the Teardrop and the Bruce, magnificent if narrow alpine trails cut in 1937 and since abandoned. They are available now to skiers willing to climb up in order to ski down—whatever their equipment. A mountain noted for its Front Four ski trails now has a Back Four, including two rediscovered by cross-country skiers. Not only are we using some of the old trails, but by looking at photographs of skiers in the 1930s—their low, stable stance utilizing extreme edging—we get a good image of the technique a cross-country skier needs for skiing down hills.

A word to alpine skiers venturing out on skinny skis. Relative to alpine equipment, cross-country gear is unforgiving on downhills. The skis are lighter, narrower, more flexible, and may or may not have metal edges; boots are ordinarily more flexible, and heels lift freely off the skis. This means less control and stability than available on alpine equipment.

But we've found that the problem is not so much equipment as misinformation and superstition. One expert alpine skier in a cross-country class protested that she couldn't do parallel turns on cross-country skis. Had she ever tried? No, but she'd often been told that they couldn't be done. Her instructor urged her to give them a try. The result, not surprisingly, was a dozen short-swing parallel turns and on-going bliss. Other alpine skiers may not have such immediate results, but they'll find they'll ski pretty much the same way on both kinds of equipment, with some subtle differences.

If you are a good alpine skier or racer, then everything you do in alpine has direct carry-over into cross-country downhill skiing. You are used to edging and unweighting radically in turns, keeping your hands low and in front, holding your upper body neutral, and getting the most out of your equipment. The strength to drive hard must be combined with flexibility. But if you are an intermediate or novice alpine skier and are used to turning by banking or swiveling, you will have to make some adjustments to be competent on skinny skis—nothing radical, a little more edging and a little more unweighting.

Modern alpine equipment permits you to turn by banking (leaning your body into the hill), with less edging, more skidding, and less emphasis on the position of the hands. Metal edges are so sharp and boots so stiff that it is not necessary to edge radically for the ski to hold and carve a turn. Since your heel is firmly attached to the ski, you can press forward and down on the top of your ski to initiate the turn with the ski tip. Loose-heeled cross-country equipment, however, allows you to press *around* a turn, but not forward and down. Further, the tip of a light cross-country ski is flexible, so you do not carve a turn on it as with an alpine ski; you turn on the midbody of the ski.

To compensate for the light equipment, your weight must be right over the center of your skis or you'll be on your rear end. It's not easy to balance on a narrow, sliding platform, especially when you are wearing what is essentially a soft running shoe attached to the ski only at the tip of the toe! Once you get balanced, the light swing weight of cross-country skis, which allows a quick edge change, is a delight.

Skiing downhill on cross-country skis is good practice for alpine skiers. No longer can you "cheat" while turning and get away with it because of the stable holding power of alpine equipment. Downhill cross-country skiing will bring you back to basics. You'll learn a tremendous amount about balance, weight, steering, and edging which is directly applicable to alpine.

The rest of this chapter moves logically from elementary to advanced turns. The pictured demonstrations are on narrow track skis. However, keep in mind that all turns can be done on all kinds of equipment.

Keep your knees bent and your hands low and in front for stability.

Body Position

Ski downhill in the ready but relaxed position you would use to receive a tennis serve, with your weight centered over your feet at all times to maintain control of your skis and to ski much longer without getting tired. (Avoid "sitting" with your rear or bending forward at your waist.) Ankles are bent and pressed forward against the top lace of the boots; this is of utmost importance because it causes the knees to flex forward as well. Flexed knees act as shock absorbers and make steering possible. As German-born instructor Adi Yoerg says, "You cannot ski with knees like the goat."

Though you flex your knees properly, if your hands are in the air (victim of an alpine hold-up?) you'll be hard-pressed to make a turn or to be secure even on a straight downhill run. Few skiers realize the importance of hand position. Your body follows your hands. Keep hands low and in front as if they are gripping bicycle handlebars. This will keep the body forward, square, and facing in the direction of the turn. Ski with your hands where you can use them easily. Hands that are too high or too far back (that is, out of your field of vision) throw you off balance.

Straight Run

Letting your skis run straight down the fall line of a slope to a natural stop as the slope flattens is a good way to get used to a bit of speed. Keep your skis hip-width apart for stability and good balance and your poles angled backward to avoid catching the stray bush or skier. Begin on a slope that is comfortable for you, getting acquainted with all the slight adjustments you have to make for bumps and ripples in the snow. This, by the way, is not just an exercise for the rankest beginner but something to return to often as you find downhill slopes on which you can simply let your skis run. In some snow conditions it is more secure to run straight with more speed than you might like than to try to pull out by turning.

Later on as you begin skiing trails, try getting all you can out of each straight downhill. You'll be amazed how much speed you can carry onto the flats. Racers occasionally attain speeds of thirty to thirty-five miles an hour, but they know the runout is safe. This is all free distance covered, normal breathing restored. Try tucking (crouching) for more speed. If your legs are fatigued, rest by keeping your legs straighter and lean over in your upper body only.

Tuck for speed.

To get up, simply roll over and forward onto your knees, then stand.

Getting Up After

When things go amiss in downhill skiing, it's usually in a delightfully big way with terrific explosions of snow. The best laughs can come from the disentangling operation after a fall. Unless you fall, you aren't trying anything new. But unless you're endowed with Neanderthal arms, you need a bit of technique to hoist yourself upright without getting uptight in the battle with gravity.

To get up from a fall, roll over onto your side so your skis are parallel, downhill from you, and across the fall line of the slope so they will not slide forward or back. If you are submerged in deep snow, forming an X with your poles will provide a stable platform from which to push off. Then simply move forward onto your knees. Your weight is now over your knees. Rock back onto your feet and stand up. No thrashing necessary!

Stepping and Skating Turns

The most obvious way to turn on cross-country skis is simply to pick one up, point in the direction you want to go, and bring the other one over next to it, in what is commonly called a step turn. It will feel a lot less awkward if you try to pick up and turn the tip of the ski rather than get the whole thing around. At first you'll feel somewhat defensive, barely able to get the skis around in time. Soon you'll be scampering, stepping quickly into or out of the tracks and around looming trees. At this point you might get a little more aggressive and indulge in accelerating skating turns, already familiar to alpine skiers and to skaters on blades and wheels.

Stepping and skating are often the only turns you can do when you are locked into deep-set machine tracks or dealing with tricky snow that catches tails and edges of skis. Little speed is lost. A single skate turn will accomplish a minimal change of direction; several skates in succession will cover a larger radius. Use skate turns to negotiate corners on the flat when your speed is fairly fast, and on downhills when your speed is not so fast that you must make a parallel carved turn.

To make a skate turn, keep your knees flexed and hands low for balance. You must edge your outside ski to give yourself a secure, nonslip platform from which to step. The critical ingredient is the weight shift from the outside ski to the inside ski. It takes a real commitment to throw your weight into the turn and to the inside. You must be able to stand on one ski, then the other, and do it quickly.

Remember not to shift weight too soon. What you're after is a definite step from one ski to the other. Most errors in making a good skate turn come from being caught in between with weight on both skis. There's simply no place for hesitation here.

Shift weight to step around.

Get a feel for your edges before heading downhill.

Edge Sense

Stopping or turning on your cross-country skis will be a lot easier if you've come to an understanding with the edges of your skis. Here are two ways to make their acquaintance.

• Stand stationary across the hill. Roll your ankles into the slope to edge your skis. Try to push your downhill ski outward (downward). It won't move if it is edged. Now flatten your downhill ski on the snow and push it outward. It will skid easily (sideslip).

• Stand across a groomed slope. Flatten both skis and sideslip down the hill. Roll your ankles and knees into the hill to edge your skis and stop. Repeat the flattening and edging several times.

Snowplow Stop

Newly sensitive to the edging of the skis, you're ready to develop some resources for stopping, unless you prefer your descents quick and free of control. The place to begin is with a snowplow.

With your knees and hands properly positioned, let your skis run downhill, then spread them apart equally into a wedge position by pressing the tails out *flat* with your heels, keeping the ski tips together. Once the tails of the skis are spread apart, rolling your ankles inward will set the skis on their inside edges, digging in sufficiently for braking. If skis are over-edged they may cross; if they are too flat they will not brake. Sink into a snowplow; bending your knees and dropping your rear will make it easier to spread skis into a wedge.

The wider the wedge and the more you edge, the slower you'll go. Keep the pressure on and you'll come to a gradual stop, not on the proverbial dime but on a string of dimes. (One thing we've found is that the snowplow is oversold as a means to put the brakes on firmly on any but the easiest

A super-wide snowplow will provide stability and maximum edging.

It's easier to start with half-plows.

downhills. To brake on a steep hill you'll have to turn up into the hill — but more on that later.)

The wider apart you hold your knees, the more effective your snowplow. Knock-knees aren't effective: bend your knees forward, not together, and keep them far enough apart to hold a beachball between them.

Half plow: A super exercise for learning the feeling of edging a ski in a snowplow is to traverse a groomed slope at an easy angle. With much of your weight on your uphill ski, push your downhill ski out into a half plow. Edge the ski to the inside to slow your speed and stop.

Straight and spread routine: This is another great exercise for getting the feel of initiating a snowplow stop. Head straight down a gentle slope with your skis parallel.

Before gaining much speed, sink and spread into a definite snowplow. But don't stop completely! Just before you lose momentum, draw your skis back parallel, gain speed, snowplow again, parallel, snowplow, and so on. Try this long enough to allow a sequence of several near-stops.

Chicken wing: Many people produce only a lopsided snowplow. Look at your tracks in the snow: both skis should be skidding, leaving a wake rather than a line. If not, correct by bringing *both* hips square to the direction you are heading so that your skis are equally weighted. Letting one hip fall back straightens that knee, makes you crooked on your skis, and leaves you with only a half-effective braking force. Arms are often the culprit here. Skiers pull elbows up and out in an imitation snowplow, hoping that the legs will, somehow, follow. Keeping your hands square and in front is a good device for squaring your hips.

WRONG! Some skiers pull elbows up and out, in an imitation snowplow, hoping the legs will follow.

Lean to the outside to steer around.

Snowplow Turn

The snowplow turn is the turn of first resort, easily initiated by putting more pressure on one ski. It is extremely stable and the foundation for more advanced turns.

To learn a snowplow turn, head downhill in your regular sliding snowplow. As you press your skis out, shift your weight and stand on the outside ski that is pointed in the direction you want to go. (Thus, in the lefthand turn shown in the photo, weight is on the right ski.) Lean to the outside of the turn as if centrifugal force were throwing you to the outside. As you put weight on this outside ski by applying heel pressure, edge it against the snow so it will hold. Steer around with your knees, always turning in the direction of the stronger ski. Lean right to turn left, like pushing a tiller away from you in a boat. Think of swooping down into a turn with your outside hand.

It's not uncommon to see a skier hurtling downhill while protesting loudly that the skis won't turn. Usually, it's caused by just a couple of errors. The skier may have put his skis on edge before getting into a snowplow. Sliding downhill on parallel rails makes it virtually impossible to come around. Remember, it's a *snowplow* turn. Think (and get into) a snowplow, then apply pressure to turn.

But keeping proper pressure on the ski is hard for those who lean into the turn. It's as if they believe that getting the brain over to the right means that the body will somehow follow. But it won't, because pressure has been taken off the left ski: they've shifted the wrong way.

From this stable position simply push in on your downhill knee to turn.

If you're having trouble with the turn, put your hands on your bent knees. (This also puts you in the proper body position.) When you want to turn, simply press in on your outside or downhill knee with your hand. Push left knee in to go right, push right knee in to go left. Feel the rhythm. Pushing on the downhill knee helps turning in three critical ways: (1) steers the downhill knee in the direction you want to turn; (2) places your weight on the downhill ski; (3) edges your downhill ski so it will carve around.

Or try this. If you want to make a right turn, imagine you're carrying a heavy suitcase (in our haunts imagine a full sap bucket) in your left hand. Let the weight pull your shoulder and arm down, putting pressure on your left ski —pressure that will make a turn.

Work from a traverse: If you are still having difficulty getting the feel for it, traverse a slope and try a partial snowplow turn up into the hill using gravity to help you stop. This is less scary and more controlled than starting by going straight downhill. Progress by doing more distinct turns from a steeper traverse.

Step to stop: Here's where you can make a snowplow turn that will really stop you on a dime in case you're hurtling downhill and come upon a skier fallen in front of you. Make a very sharp, emphatic snowplow turn up into the side of the trail and step the uphill ski over next to the downhill steering ski with a motion like your old high school two-step dance. This is really a natural finish to a snowplow turn and is the gateway to parallel skiing, giving you a feeling of completing turns with maximum control. After all, your uphill ski isn't doing much in the turn — stepping emphatically off it will swing you around faster. Be sure to bend your knees to absorb the rapid deceleration.

Linking Your Turns

Turns downhill are actually easier when more than one is done, so that the ending of one turn sets you up for the next, establishing a rhythm and cadence that blends the individual ingredients of turning into one flowing motion. Once you learn the ABCs of doing a snowplow, skate, stem christie, parallel, or telemark turn, try to link several together. This is what skiing is really about: negotiating the slope as if all your turns were tied to each other. "She can really crank her skis right and left" is truly a complimentary way of saying someone is a good skier.

Stem Christie

The stem christie is a faster, more definite and prettier turn than a snowplow. It moves you toward a parallel while maintaining the security of the snowplow. It's a good braking turn, because you can jam the tails of your skis into the snow.

Begin with your skis parallel and traverse the hill at a forty-five degree angle. Push or step out with the unweighted uphill ski to form a wedge. Thus, in starting the lefthand turn shown here, the right ski is pushed out. Complete this snowplow part of the turn two-thirds of the way around in a controlled skid. Now bring your skis parallel by gradually shifting or stepping your weight completely over to the outside (downhill) ski so that the inside ski comes in effortlessly. In this position, traverse the hill parallel in preparation for the next turn. By bringing your skis parallel at the end of the turn, you learn to pick up one ski and float it so that you're not always on both skis as you are in the snowplow.

For your first stem-christie turns, snowplow across the fall line, then close your skis, bringing them parallel. Your wedge will get narrower as you get better. Gradually reduce the snowplow part of the turn as your balance improves, and start the skidding action sooner. Now you're bringing your skis parallel earlier and moving toward parallel skiing, leaving behind the wedge.

Now bring your ski parallel
after your snowplow turn.

Parallel Turn

You don't necessarily have to do parallel turns to be a competent skier on cross-country skis. But if you're comfortable with stem christies, parallel turns are only a short slide away and will give you more control through a faster, tighter turn. Despite what you may have heard, you do not have to be an alpine skier to learn to ski parallel. We've often seen beginning skiers produce a parallel turn instead of the intended stem christie or, rarely, snowplow turns. Here's how:

Work from a platform: In linked parallel turns, speed is checked by setting the edges at the completion of each turn. This is done by a sharp pushing of the heels down into the snow and an acute flexing of the knees forward and sideways into the hill. This sharp interruption of your momentum from your edge set creates a rebound which makes unweighting for the next turn easier. At the same time, a hard pole plant and forward thrust with the downhill pole also helps this rebound. Sink with your knees and plant your poles to trigger the turn.

Place your weight: For your knees to do the job, you'll need an assist from properly placed body weight. To keep weight on your downhill ski you'll have to lean out and over it, that is, away from, not into, the hill even while your knees are driving into the hill. In this way you avoid banking your turns like a water skier—a habit which usually leads to falls on cross-country skis.

Release your weight: To get weight off both skis, spring up and forward to release the edge and free the skis in order to steer them around. Now that the skis are unweighted, a change of direction is possible and the skis will run to the fall line. It's like pushing in the clutch on an automobile. Once the friction is released, you can shift gears. (In skiing, it's a shift of edges that you're after.)

Change direction: Press forward and down on your skis with knees steering in the new direction. The pressure down and forward that builds during the turn controls the tips of the skis. The harder the pressure, the sharper the turn. Notice the change in the ski edges coming through the turn, the push downward with the heels, and the outside hand driving in the direction of the turn. Knees are

A

B

(A) Work from a platform to set up for the turn. (B) Unweight to release your edges. (C) Press down and forward to steer around. (D) Get set for the next turn.

C

D

bent, especially the outside one, and weight has been transferred mostly to the downhill ski. Concentrate on keeping the knee of the downhill leg bent for maximum steering and edging. To edge, point knees to the inside of the turn, angling them into the hill.

At first, it may help you to think of merely "standing" on the downhill ski to turn, changing direction with a step- ping motion. Eventually you'll want the skis more equally weighted for better stability and edging. Use both legs together and really roll your knees into the turn to steer. Flexed knees provide the torque to turn.

At the end, the turn is finished with the skis both pressed against the snow and set for the next. During the whole process, shoulders have faced down the hill.

Pole properly: At this point in the anatomy lesson one should pause to find out a little more about hands and poles. The hands are really beginning the turn. You are essentially turning around your downhill pole, and plant- ing it decisively is a way of saying "get ready" to turn your skis. Reaching out with your hand keeps your body cen- tered and over your skis, ready as you initiate the turn. Planting the pole makes you solid to begin the turn. It serves as a steadying point. Keep driving that downhill hand forward throughout the turn, or you will ski past your pole, twisting your body back and out of position and reduc- ing the bite of your edges on the snow. If you're having a hard time getting from one turn to the other, check your hands.

While your downhill hand is planting the pole, what is your other hand doing? If it is lazy and has drifted back past your hip, it will be hard to bring the skis around for your next turn. No matter which hand is planting the pole, they should both be out to the side and in front (within your field of vision) as if you were embracing an enormous snowman or holding the handlebars of a grossly oversized bicycle so that you'll be square on your skis for easier and quicker turns.

For those who have had the distinction of learning to ski downhill after years of cross-country, there is a functional difference in using long cross-country poles for doing alpine-style turns. The shorter alpine poles, planted verti- cally, bring you forward onto your skis. Plant a cross-

Rhythm makes one turn into an enjoyable series.

country pole vertically and your hand will be so high that your weight will be thrown back off your skis. If you are doing only lift-served skiing on your sticks, use a shorter pole (but don't expect as much out of your diagonal stride or double poling as you're heading for the lift). When using a normal length cross-country pole you must recreate the short pole feeling. You'll probably find that you have to cock your wrist, getting the hand forward and the basket way out in front of the pole plant.

Cross-country racing poles with butterfly baskets tend to skitter off hard snow when planted. If you have to use them, turn them around so the half basket points forward for long downhill runs in off track skiing.

Maintain rhythm: Maintaining your rhythm is essential when making linked parallel turns. Allow one turn to lead into the next, making you feel as if you're "bouncing" from left to right as you turn down the slope. Your decisive yet smooth pole plant sets your rhythm. Remember to keep your upper body quiet and facing mostly downhill throughout the turns as your legs turn under you. This is called anticipation, for you are anticipating the next turn. Look ahead far enough so you can set your moves and timing. If your head doesn't swivel, your body won't, either. For a little help here, station a friend downhill and keep your eyes on him or her as you make your turns.

To get the feeling of how twisting at the waist will help to start each turn, mountain guide Allan Bard suggests standing stationary across the hill. Turn your upper body and look straight down the fall line. Put your pole in the snow. Now, pick up your downhill ski, transmitting the spring-like twist in your waist to the ski, causing it to turn.

Breaking-your-tail-loose exercise: To get the feeling of starting a turn with your skis together, traverse a slope, sink, and as you start to rise up, turn up into the hill by pushing the tails of your skis down the hill, or breaking them loose. Try this from progressively steeper traverses and greater speed.

Hockey-stop exercise: Here you're breaking the tails loose more emphatically, carrying a little more speed as you ski down the fall line. The photo sequence shows "crouching" or unweighting the skis, rising up to unweight the skis, and quickly turning the skis across the fall line in a skidding stop just as you'd stop on hockey skates. The skis skid sideways and bite into the snow hard to stop crisply. The hockey stop also works effectively as an emergency stop when someone skis in front of you unexpectedly or you discover that a stream has cut across a trail during late spring skiing.

Hockey stop: this will get you
to turn on your skis quickly.

Snowplow-shortswing: this helps you loosen up your knees and feel the rhythm of linked turns.

Snowplow-shortswing exercise: This exercise develops the rhythm of linked turns and is the best connector of turns that we've yet found. It forces you to flex your knees to steer your skis. If you can do this one, we guarantee you can do parallel turns!

Head straight down a gentle slope in a *shallow* snowplow, and from this narrow wedge do quick and continuously linked turns. As soon as your weight comes onto one ski and you start to turn, get off that ski and onto the other and turn in that direction. Think of it as making decisive half turns. This teaches rhythm, edge change, weight shift, some rebounding, steering in the knees, and a pole plant. As you master this, progressively bring the skis together more and move into parallel skiing.

Imitation is an excellent teacher here. Follow another skier closely and stay in his tracks so you imitate and feel the rhythm and bounce.

Speeding without Spilling

Even the most competent ski swivelers get into situations where turns will not be the order of the day. The time will come when you simply have to ride it out. High speeds don't necessarily have to be terrifying (indeed they may become addictive).

If you want to hang on in high-speed bombing, hands should be positioned low and in front to maintain a lower body position (like an opened up tuck), ankles and knees flexed for steerage and to act as shock absorbers, feet apart for stability, and weight directly over your skis. It's as if you're rising up slightly out of the downhill racer's tuck, extending your hands forward and to the side. If you're hurtling through a sweeping corner, stay in this position and steer with your hands, driving the outside hand in the direction of the turn. To get a feeling for the hand drive and

Stay low and forward when bombing.

weight shift, try it when you're stationary on the flat. Drive your left arm and hand forward and feel the weight come onto your left leg and ski. At high speeds this will pull you around a right turn as long as you stay low, keeping your arm out front as well as down. Dragging your poles, especially the inside one, like outriggers will give more stability, but be careful not to snag baskets on a branch or root.

The feeling of speed on any kind of skis is a real charge. Once you feel it, you're hooked, a hopeless speed junkie. In the Sun Valley Pin Binding Downhill, several hundred skiers hurtle 3,400 vertical feet in times of a bit over three minutes. Ned accepted an invitation to run three pins at the Speed Skiing Qualifications in Colorado in 1983. Sporting it was, and although others have gone faster elsewhere, he quite enjoyed a sprint on the skinnies at 61.798 miles an hour.

Falling

In pursuit of downhill competence, falling is inevitable. While it is much more likely to happen in the hills, it can, of course, occur on the flats: consider the ski-stopping shred of birchbark in the tracks. Or the infrequently seen errant pole plant that puts the basket solidly over the tip of a ski, an entanglement from which recovery is virtually impossible.

Face it; as skiers we've all fallen and will fall again. With little choice in the matter, let us relax and not let it get in the way of our continuing efforts to be better or go faster on our skis. Looked at as failure, falling will only make you miserable. We've all seen the skier who wipes out and, embarrassed by the abrupt intersection of rear and snow, jumps instantly to his feet, quickly brushing off the snow, and takes a covert look around to see who might have witnessed. Or the beginning skier in a class who grimly mutters after a tumble, "That's the third one." But for the skier who's airborne, en route to the inevitable crater, who realizes that he's been indulging in, as Thomas McGuane puts it, "a bravura extension beyond his own abilities," the fall merely marks forward progress (emphasis on bravura).

Not only will falling become less onerous, it may become downright addictive. You'll relish the chance for display

First the pole plant, then the face plant.

and pay more attention to style. No longer satisfied with a simple sit down, you'll hope for something more flamboyant. Going for more speed will allow for a Flying Buttocks Arrest ("Parallel Bun Stop," for more advanced skiers). If the density of the snowpack is right, a Thundering Buttocks Arrest can be achieved. Points may be awarded for flagrant travel over the tips of the skis, for securing maximum air time, for devastation of equipment, and for pruning and removal of shrubs and trees.

Worried about falling in front of others? Soon you'll long for an onlooker to substantiate claims made later for distance of air travel. Or for a witness to a windmilling, seemingly endless, high-speed gainer, through whom you can relive the flailing and burrowing. For you, for all of us, there will be that giddy moment when time seems to have stopped, when we're weightless, free, arcing over the tips of our skis, dead certain that we're about to bury our heads.

Telemark Downhill

It is not uncommon to ride the lifts at a downhill resort these days and hear fellow riders calling out "Telemark!" to genuflecting rover packs of cross-country skiers charging down the slopes below. What they're asking for is a turn that's been around ever since skis were twelve feet long and attached to the shoes with thongs. Unlike other turns, in which feet are kept side by side, in the telemark a skier scissors the legs fore and aft, steering around on what is essentially one long ski. It's a graceful, flamboyant turn, the mark of the all-around cross-country stylist, and the only one you can't also do with alpine skis. This is the turn that makes the most of a loose heel.

It was in Norway, in the mid-1800s, that Sondre Norheim first wrapped twisted osier withes around his heel to gain more steering control, thus "inventing" the binding. From 1868 on, he and the ruffians from the Telemark region in southern Norway dominated ski competitions in Christiania (now Oslo) as the turn that Norheim developed in Telemark overshadowed the skidding, parallel Christiania turn. A half century ago modern alpine bindings that clamped heels to skis spelled the eclipse of the telemark turn, but only temporarily. Even as late as 1946, a ski manual stated, "Because of its narrow track and the minimum amount of snow displacement, the telemark requires less physical effort in deep snow than any other turn. This factor alone justifies its presence in a skier's bag of tricks."

The recent revival of the telemark is partly due to the switch-hitting of some of the best alpine skiers and partly to the introduction of more sophisticated metal-edged cross-country skis with alpine-like flexes and stiff boots. And the turn itself has changed a bit. No longer does the tip of the back ski passively nestle next to the instep of the front boot. The ski is still back but more nearly parallel, and carving. A top-notch telemark turn is aggressive, like a good alpine turn. Alpine, nordic, and mountaineering skiers alike have rediscovered the challenge, usefulness, and just plain fun of sweeping downhill leaving a single carved track.

Why Telemark?

Aside from the utility of the turn, telemarks have a low-rider appeal. As Todd Eastman of Stowe, Vermont, says, "the lower you get, the deeper the snow." What we're after is low-rider enjoyment. If a parallel is an upright turn, then the telemark is a downright turn—downright fun! Telemark anywhere, just because it feels good. Or be offhand about it: we've seen members of the University of Vermont cross-country ski team telly to a stop at the end of an interval training loop, instead of braking, as most skiers would, with a parallel hockey stop.

But a telemark is useful as well as fun; use it when you need fore and aft stability. In deep powder? Drop into a telemark, essentially putting yourself in one long ski for power steering par excellence. Frozen in a vice-like grip with your parallel stance in dense crud snow? Initiate a telemark with a step or two, or even a jump. It's quick. So too in tight trees. Even moguls. It's stable. No wonder ski jumpers land in a telemark position. If you're carrying a backpack, a smooth telly will not throw you down. It's a tolerant turn, this double-clutch shuffle, custom tailored for cross-country equipment.

And custom tailored for people like Jan Reynolds of Stowe, Vermont, with whom Gillette has shared his last three expeditions. In China Jan set the high-altitude skiing record for women: 24,757 feet. She'll attack any slope and any snow condition but does so with calculated caution, since she's dislocated both shoulders, both elbows, and has chronic knee problems. The telemark allows her to ski it all.

Cross-country downhill has put a new spark into skiing, an uninhibited, fall-down-and-get-up-and-go spirit. It's a pure delight to swing with gravity on light equipment, switching from parallel to telemark as the terrain and snow dictate, just as we'd intermingle diagonal and double-pole strides on the flat track.

Before You Arc

Here are two budding telemarkers overheard at a break-fast in a diner in Bishop, California. First woman: "When I finally stepped out on that forward ski and really committed, it felt great." Second woman: "Yeah, same here, and when I dropped the stem and got those skis closer together, slicing one arc, yum."

Skiing downhill is by no means a natural sport. It is not like walking, running, jumping, or throwing. It is very much a learned activity, one that takes sophisticated concentration and coordination. All our instincts tell us not to fall, not to lean out over the skis, not to speed. But, like the Bishop women, we can all get the hang of it if we focus on the essentials. Of all skiing skills, the telemark turn is perhaps the hardest commonly executed maneuver. The balance demanded at first seems that of a tightrope walker, the body position that of a rock star in the layout position, and the velocity that of a downhill racer—all on cross-country skis that look, to the neophyte, rather insubstantial in comparison to their obese alpine cousins. ("Why are my skis so thin?" said a friend of ours, responding to a question from an alpine skier. "Madam, they've been sick.")

Chances are that you will have had some skiing expertise under your belt before you try your first telemark. As a cross-country skier, you must learn to entertain more speed and learn to carve through a turn. If you're an alpine skier, you must adjust to a different body position. Even though the body position may initially feel weird, the rhythm of the turns will be natural. You are working to overcome a mind problem more than a physical problem. Use the local ski area lifts to get mileage and to get accustomed to accelerating straight over into the fall line, to capture an easy balance, to turn left and right with equal expertise, and to prime those thigh muscles.

Telemark virtuoso Art Burrows of Aspen, Colorado, advises, "If you make a commitment, as I did a few years ago, to try to ski everything on cross-country skis, then you will get good. Then you will not have the alternative of retreating to alpine skis when it looks tough. You will press through and get better."

Body Position

A telemark is really only a super-duper, gravity-assisted diagonal stride. Head down to your local bowling alley and roll a set. The position you find yourself in as you release the ball is a hardwood telly. Position on your skis is the key ingredient when learning. Quick turns will come later.

Weight even: Distribute your weight fifty-fifty between the front and back ski. The half of your weight on your rear ski is going to feel like eighty percent at first. Think of squashing a bug under the *ball* of your back foot. (Avoid being up on tiptoe, making it impossible to exert pressure, and leading to tepid telemarking.) Pressure here will make the rear ski edge and carve instead of skid, giving rudder-like control. Beginners are apt to do the D'Artagnan, lunging forward onto a bent front leg, back leg straight, as if skewering a seventeenth century opponent.

Proper body position is a fifty-fifty proposition.

WRONG! Don't do the D'Artagnan.

Body aligned: Bend at the knees, not at the waist. To be centered over your skis means standing more erect than in alpine or flat-track cross-country skiing. Viewed from the side, a telemarker's shoulder, hip, and knee of the flexed back leg should be in a straight line. Keep your head up. Your body follows your head, so a droopy cranium hunches your upper body, transferring too much weight onto the front ski. Better to drive your hips in under you.

WRONG! Hunching puts too much weight onto the front ski.

Feet snugged up: Keep your feet fairly close together fore and aft at first, concentrating on knee bending. Feet working closely will feel familiar to alpine skiers and will prove easier for all beginning Telemarkers to weight the skis equally. Touch the trailing knee to the calf of the leading leg to avoid too long a spread. Never allow your rear leg to straighten.

Hands low: Ratify the Neutrality Act between Legs and Upper Body, securing an enduring Peace of the Torso. Keep it quiet up top, especially with a backpack, hands low for optimum center of gravity. Balance is difficult at first. You'll tend to lift up your hands and jab your poles in busily to stay upright, looking like a great square-rigged ship. Well and good to use outriggers as a training crutch, but this banging about will upset your rhythm, expend lots of energy, and eliminate any aggressiveness. Collapse that umbrella you appear to be holding over your head and let yourself down on your skis. To quiet your arms, think of gripping the handles of your poles lightly. To get your arms low when learning, consider using very short poles, some twenty centimeters shorter than normal.

Drive the inside hand: Concentrate on driving the arm opposite the forward leg to keep you square on your skis. It is a compensating factor for the rear leg. When you turn, hold the inside (uphill) hand dynamically forward to offset centrifugal force and to cancel a tendency to overrotate (the forward ski a too heavily weighted pivot point) and spin around crazily at the end of each turn. Remember your diagonal stride, the dynamics of which are retained by thrusting your hips through. Commit to the turn, then sink and weight both skis.

(Top) RIGHT! Drive the inside hand. *(Bottom)* WRONG! When hands get back, a fall is often ahead.

First Turn

For the time being, forget about your poles.

1. Standing in place, familiarize yourself with the telemark position by sliding your skis back and forth like a diagonal stride, bending your knees and switching the lead ski. Discover that your weight feels best when equal on both skis.

2. Time to move. Stride slightly downhill across an easy, groomed slope in the familiar rhythm of your diagonal stride, sinking into a telemark position with each stride. After three or four strides, push your *downhill* ski forward, genuflect, and do one turn up into the slope. Repeat, making a garland.

Garland.

Pressing into a turn.

3. Turn down the hill. This will involve a bit more speed. Once again stride across the hill in a shallow traverse. This time slide your *uphill* ski forward, stand on its inside edge, genuflect, press on both skis continually, and steer all the way around through the fall line with your front knee. There's your first real telemark.

Remember the two keys: (a) fifty percent of your weight on the rear foot; (b) drive the inside hand. Do these, and you'll elude half the telemark's sitzmarks. A loose-heeled binding means you cannot exert forward pressure on the tip of the ski, as in alpine, so you must sit squarely on the skis and use the maximum sidecut underfoot for turning. Pressure the ski into doing the work for you. Skis must really bend to turn—a curved object tends to follow an arced path.

Bunny hop.

Bunny-hop exercise: Can't get that feeling of committing into the turn? Wayne Hansen of Jackson, Wyoming, gets his students to bunny hop. Traversing across an easy slope, they hop up into the air and land in a telemark stance. On each rhythmical hop they switch ski leads. Finally, on the third or fourth hop, they land and, in the same motion, press around in a telemark turn.

Rock and roll exercise: Your first telemark may be a project on the skids, sliding out rather than carving. You have to get driving thrust out onto the front ski, then follow with a quick rock back and drop down with weight on the rear ski to edge through the turn. Here's an exercise to get the feeling: during a shallow traverse line across the hill, put your weight (as you normally would) on the downhill ski. Now pick the tip of the uphill ski up off the snow, then step forward and around into the fall line. (By lifting the *tip* of the ski, it rocks you back enough to force a concentration of weight onto the back ski so it will carve.) Sink and press through the turn, allowing the rear ski to come in close to the steering front ski, riding them both. Rocking back puts weight on the rear ski. The roll forward catapults you into the turn. The step brings you through the fall line quickly, controlling speed. In the turn, both skis are weighted and carving a single arc, and hips are thrust into the turn.

Rock and roll.

Stepping to initiate a turn.

Stepping out: We like the idea of stepping to initiate the turn at first. (Later you'll use it for short, quick turns in crud snow and steep terrain.) It commits your front foot to the turn and briefly utilizes the familiar stability of a wedge. Think of driving that front ski like a diagonal stride. But as soon as the turn takes place, weight the feet equally. Squeeze down onto that back foot smoothly so the rear ski becomes useful in edging and carving for control. Think of pressing down the *little toe* of the rear foot. This automatically edges the back ski. Using the rear ski makes the telemark useful as well as pretty.

Knee guards and safety straps: Give your rear leg a bit of consideration now that your knee is cranked down close to the snow. A hidden rock or stump can devastate an innocent knee cap. Wear basketball knee pads for protection if you're going to go for any amount of speed. And use safety straps to prevent a runaway ski should the binding release.

Speed for Ease

For long radius telemarks on groomed slopes and in light powder, you don't need the step once you get used to the acceleration. It actually gets easier with speed, but you have got to put yourself in the fall line and love it. "You must attain the maximum velocity to create the necessary resistance," deadpans Art Burrows, "then just stand there and arc. It's truly energy conserving." With speed, you just cruise, gently rising up and down with each turn, edging in alternate directions as you shift skis fore and aft. Speed allows a more parallel telemark. Slower telemarks are more like a stem maneuver.

Shift weight early: The key for these long, steered turns without a step is pressing more weight on the back ski as speed increases. Timing is critical. Start shifting your weight onto the inside ski just before the turn. Otherwise you'll get on what will be the rear ski too late. You'll lose the carving power of the rear ski, and the turn will be dead.

Staying in a wedge invites a fall.

Cut the stem: As speed and confidence increase, cut down the angle (stemming stance) between the skis, so they slice. To do this, increase the radius or speed of the turn, or initiate it from a parallel stance. Staying in a wedge too long during the turn means each ski follows a different arc, cancelling the steering action. When the wedge is eliminated, the telemark becomes truly a steered turn.

Pole plant: With long-radius high-speed steered turns, less unweighting is needed, so it is not necessary to plant your poles. Just shift ski lead, lean into the turn, and go with the speed. But you'll want to plant the downhill pole when doing sharper, quicker telemarks, thereby creating a stable platform from which to rise up, unweight, and roll your knees to start the turn. It initiates the lead change of the skis. Plant the pole so it is synced with this briefly parallel and compact stance. Planting the pole also sets you facing down the hill with your upper body coiled, or torqued, in anticipation of the coming turn.

Plant pole for quick turns.

No-poles-barred exercise: Keeping yourself facing generally down the hill makes turning quicker and prevents overrotation. Twisting at the waist also automatically weights and edges the rear ski so it will carve for you early in the turn and not leave you behind. To get the sensation of facing downhill and anticipating, hold your poles in front as a tightrope walker would, then make several turns, trying to keep the poles across the hill at all times.

No-poles-barred.

Breathing-in-breathing-out exercise: Todd Eastman would ask you to exaggerate your breathing to get through a turn. Inhale as you come into the turn. This raises you a little off your skis (unweighting to initiate). Exhale as you sink into the turn. Think of everything dropping down, getting heavier as buoyant air is expelled.

Reach-not-for-the-sky exercise: Especially on harder snow, you'll want to thrust, or flex, your knees sideways into the hill to steer and edge. Compensate by bending your upper body out, away from the hill and over your feet in a comma shape. Your weight is then directly on your feet, yet ski edges are biting. Now if you hit a slick icy spot, your skis will not fly out from under you as they might if you banked the turn. To get the feel of this body position, Rick Borkovec of Crested Butte, Colorado, one of the country's earliest telemark practitioners, suggests pressing the downhill (outside) hand in and down, toward the heel of the back foot to feel the angled body position.

Reach-not-for-the-sky.

Linked telemark turns.

Linking Your Turns

Ultimately aim for connecting several turns. It is the *rhythm* of telemarking that skiers find exquisitely natural, like the smooth grace of the diagonal stride, one motion leading into the next. Linking makes your turns not only easier but more dynamic and utilitarian in all types of snow. Long, hesitant traverses between turns destroys cadence and strains your thigh muscles. The beauty lies in repeating the arc. Above all, follow gravity and red-line the fun meter.

Telemark Racing

Competition is the logical extension of most sporting pastimes, and telemarking is no exception. In the late 1970s a group of exalpine racers in Colorado, already expert backcountry telemarkers, established the Summit Telemark Series. Wool knickers, touring boots, and long, deep sweeping tellies were the order of the day.

Today the standards of competition have risen drastically. The best racers look like aggressive Alpine World Cup champions and practice their gates daily. Races are held throughout the country. The spectator no longer sees any wool. Sleek nylon racing suits, refurbished leather alpine boots (some with plastic reinforcements and buckles) and metal-edged skis with alpine flex characteristics specifically designed for racing are typical. Even with these serious accouterments, telemark racing has kept its fun-loving, know-everyone-else-on-the-circuit atmosphere.

Races are run on dual giant slalom courses, with elimination rounds, competitors going head-to-head. Races average forty seconds, with the best women running only one and a half to two seconds behind the men. In the final Summit Series race in 1982, less than two seconds separated the first fifteen men after two runs.

The rules of telemark racing require that the racer *execute* his turn as a telemark (no matter how brief). He is not required to pass through the gate in a telemark. Most good racers have completed their turn above the gate. They hit an instantaneous, sharply powerful telemark, then fire on in a parallel position until the next turn. Gatekeepers

Vern Twombly running a gate in the
North American Championships.

assess one-second penalties for each nontelemark turn.

The speed of the top guns is utterly fantastic. But even
with speed and jamming turns, they ski smoothly, careful
not to get too far forward, even though racing elicits a
tendency to lean into the course and off that carving, rear
ski.

Although high-level racing is attractive for only a select
few, it is a valid and exciting part of cross-country skiing.
Running gates, regardless of the speed you wish to go,
improves your skiing. It helps your ability to turn at will,
putting you more in control. It keeps you honest: everything must be precisely executed at higher speeds and
higher pulse rates.

6

Coping with Terrain

Skiing smoothly over varied terrain is one of cross-country skiing's really sensual pleasures, a way of getting clear of gravity and using it to your advantage. It's instinctive skiing on the trail that we all strive for: a combination of technique, strength, and mental attitude. It comes only with experience. The kind of refinements that allow you to ski successfully through any kind of terrain and snow condition don't lend themselves easily to textbook analysis. For example, we can't tell you when to stem into a downhill turn and when to step out of it, but only that the two can be combined as terrain dictates. The best we can do

Varied terrain offers a challenge to cross-country skiers.

is to suggest some possibilities of dealing with terrain, leaving the refinements to your growing skills. They'll come quickly if you're willing to go back over a section of trail that may literally have thrown you, and if you stay alert to tracks left by preceding skiers. Have they skated around a turn or skidded? On uphills, have they herringboned or tackled the grade straight up?

One thing for certain: you'll want to be looking well ahead as you're skiing. With your eyes glued resolutely to your skis, you'll find the trail full of unsettling surprises rather than opportunities for smooth skiing.

Tracks

In machine-set tracks, you won't have much opportunity to stop unless you lift one ski outside of the track and form a half snowplow. The trick is to not put the brakes on too quickly. Many beginners will simply jam a ski out into the snow and find themselves pitched forward by the abrupt deceleration. It is better to keep more of your weight over the ski that is still in the track and ease onto your braking and plowing ski, increasing the amount of edge and pressure to bring yourself to a stop. (Use this half plow to slow your speed on sidehill traverses by standing on the uphill ski that is going straight and plowing with the lower ski, a secure maneuver in troublesome terrain and awkward snow.)

Aging tracks heavily traveled by skiers can turn from aids to obstacles. Sometimes it's the railroad switchyard effect as one track blends into the other for a few feet. Look ahead and plan for this. Nimble skiing is at a premium here. Get off the ski that is headed for trouble so that it will float as the other ski carries you through the distinct channel. Sometimes both tracks disappear, and here you stand securely on both skis, double-poling rather than diagonal-striding. If it is a really slippery section, put both skis on their inside edges for added security and guidance.

The easiest flat or uphill corner isn't a corner at all but merely a bend in the track. Try to ski around it by feathering the tip of the outside ski (swinging it around the front of the other ski in a pigeon-toed action), instead of lifting skis out and clomping around. This demands some delicate heel-toe maneuvering.

Steer through fast downhills.

On a fast downhill curve, a track usually will not have been set in the first place, or if it has, it will be quickly plowed out and a rut or bank skied into the outside of the curve. Try to ride this bank like a bobsled, driving your outside hand and outside ski into the turn to help steer you around.

If you are heading downhill in a machine-set track, you can usually ride the track around gradual corners by steering with your knees. Moving the outside ski forward a bit aids steering power. Remember to push your rear into the turn, or centrifugal force will pop you off the tracks and into the snowbank. To aid stability drag the inside pole on the snow as an outrigger. If the corner is fast or sharp, step out of the track with your inside ski, letting it ride straight. This gives you a wider, more secure stance while your outside ski is still stable in the track, steering you around the corner.

It is not uncommon to find bumpy, undulating flat and uphill sections of trail, especially early in the season when snow cover is sparse in the woods. The question is, How do you ski smoothly through these bumps when only part of your ski is touching the snow? Let your ski ride up the bump, then kick off the backside, using it like a sprinter's block so you get an extra burst of speed and keep up your momentum. The precise timing of a hurdler is what you are after. To hit a bump just right for maximum push, you must look ahead and be constantly adjusting the length of your stride so that you push just after your foot goes over the crest, perhaps taking an extra-long stride or a delicate half-stride at times.

Some bumps may be so big that you'll want to break up your diagonal striding routine with one or two double poles off the top, thus carrying more speed off the downhill. An experienced skier makes sure to double-pole off the downside of the bump, using gravity to the greatest advantage.

Once over a bump you may find yourself in a dip. Try to get through without imitating a suspension bridge, which will result in a decided lack of kick and glide and possibly a broken ski. To negotiate dips of less than a ski length, slide one ski tip into the bottom of the hollow. Then, in one long stride, shoot the other ski across to the other side of the dip. This gives you two advantages: (1) no bridging; (2) a solid kick forward off the slope of the dip (sprinter's block). To negotiate dips of greater width, simply double-pole through, making sure your knees are flexed and weight is over your feet.

A moderately rolling downhill section well endowed with bumps gives an amusement park air to cross-country skiing. If you are just getting acquainted with skiing, soak up the bumps with your legs while keeping your upper body quiet. As you hit the bump, be ready to be pitched forward; compensate by flexing your legs and leaning back just a bit, or assume a telemark position. Bumpy trails may give rollercoaster thrills but are not always rollercoaster smooth, so you may find one knee near your chest while the other is almost straight. So use independent leg action as an auto uses independent shock absorbers to smooth out the ride on a rough road, allowing you to make tiny adjustments to keep your skis on the snow.

Skiing off a steep slope onto the flat tends to pitch you forward. To guard against this, sit back just a bit as you encounter the transition and be ready to soak up the deceleration with your legs. Better yet, don't take it straight on but ski diagonally onto the flat. The most dramatic transition is that which ski jumpers encounter on landing. Like them, you might want to use the telemark position for maximum fore-and-aft stability.

Bumps can be a natural aid to turning. Use the top of the bump as a pivot point around which to swivel your skis, sliding off the backside. Finally, if you don't soak up the bump, it will send you into the air, a condition often sought by more experienced and playful skiers who have checked the warranty on their skis. While you are airborne, you'll want to remain relaxed and keep your weight over your skis, lowering your legs for landing and to absorb the shock of impact. We used to jump on cross-country skis on the twenty-meter hill during high school days. It was a gas, but a great depleter of team equipment!

Off Track

Extreme uphills: Going up steep slopes can be as tedious as downhill can be thrilling. Look at the slope carefully, trying to pick out the most logical route around obstacles. Instead of butting heads with the hills straight on, consider traversing back and forth on a manageable angle, especially if you're breaking trail in deep snow or carrying a heavy backpack. If you have to sidestep, modify your technique so you step up and forward each time.

When the snow is like deep yogurt, breaking trail can be tough. Let the ski ride on top of the snow as you stride forward instead of physically picking it up. Be more emphatic about setting your ski on the soft snow for more grip. Neither a plodder nor a racer be: keep up a steady shuffling gait—it's less laborious than thrashing and bashing. Get your shoulders into the act for maximum pole extension.

Give serious consideration to the use of climbing skins in off-trail skiing if you face long uphill climbs of hundreds of vertical feet. These pieces of artificial sealskin give foolproof grip up even the sharpest inclines, thus saving valuable energy because the fight is taken out of the climb. Modern skins hook over ski tips and stick to ski bottoms. They stick better if the ski is dry. Swab adhesive on the smooth side of the skin, and they are ready for several applications. At the top of the climb, you can remove them without taking off your skis. Flip one ski up behind you so the tip is on the ground. Reach back and strip the skin. Double each skin, stick it to itself, and toss it in your pocket or backpack. Now you're ready for a fast downhill run on skis free of climbing wax. You're ahead both uphill and down!

Skins should be wide enough to reach nearly to the edges of your ski bottoms for maximum grabbing surface. Make sure they do not cover the edge of the ski, for when it is icy you may need to sidestep, biting with the edge. (A way to improvise climbers in an emergency is to weave small diameter rope over and under the length of the ski, in effect putting chains on your skis.)

When traversing sidehills on softer snows, you have to fight the desire to edge the ski radically for apparent security. Rather, you must have the full width of the skin on the snow for the best traction, which means keeping your knee directly over the ski instead of turning into the slope. As the grade steepens, keep your head up for a better body position so your weight is more directly over your feet. Don't lean into the hill, bringing on slippage. Resist the urge to punch your ski into the snow for more secure grip. You risk collapsing the snow under your ski. Instead, apply steady, gentle pressure. You must be extraordinarily careful when traversing steep, icy slopes because the thickness of the skin and hairs tend to lift the edge of the ski off the snow, possibly leading to a dangerous slide.

Ned Gillette has used skins on all his recent expeditions. They provide secure snow trekking under heavy loads. During the three hundred-mile traverse of Pakistan's Karakoram Himalaya, he left the skins attached for short downhill runs in soft snows. This provided a slow, secure descent while carrying one hundred and twenty pounds on cross-country skis at altitudes up to 22,500 feet. In retrospect, Ned finds it hard to believe that his team, purists all, used wax during the five-hundred-mile ski expedition

Skins were frequently used on Ned Gillette's Karakoram traverse.

across Ellsmere Island in the Canadian Arctic. Each man pulled a sled with two hundred and forty pounds of provisions. What a boon skins would have been! We live and learn.

Steep downhills: Just because you are at the top of an intimidatingly steep slope or headwall, don't lose your cool. Even as a novice you already have all the technical moves necessary to descend fairly steep slopes. The width of the pitch will determine what you can get away with. Wide-open western slopes lend themselves to long traverses linked by kick turns or sidestepping. Take the slow and easy approach by seeking out the path of least resistance and utilizing these familiar techniques.

On steep traverses resist the urge to lean into the hill.

Whether you are turning or traversing on steep terrain, it is vital to lean out from the hill so your weight is over your feet while you drive your knees into the hill so your ski edges will grip. Ned at last completely understood this feeling of leaning away from what seems secure while traversing steep icy slopes in the Sierra, carrying a heavy backpack. Unless he consciously forced himself to lean far away from the slope, his mountaineering skis with climbing skins attached would begin to slip, which might have led to a dangerous fall as he crossed above a line of cliffs.

If you are unsure of changing directions by snowplow or parallel turn, remember old trusty, the kick turn. This is the easiest way to link your traverses. When you want to slow down at the end of your traverse, simply point your skis up into the hill and stop, or use the half snowplow. Set yourself securely on the snow (it's hoped you've found a little platform which is more level), and kick around as quickly as possible. You don't want to hesitate while standing with one ski up in the air, precariously perched.

Remember that you don't have to go straight down, make turns, or even go across that steep slope. Sidestepping and sideslipping are secure because you are using the full length of your ski edges to grip the snow. You can stand stationary as long as you wish and descend at your discretion. Use the same body position as for traversing.

Steep chutes can present grave problems, especially in the tree-shrouded East. They are usually narrow, and frequently packed hard by previous skiers, and very fast. It is often difficult to check your speed. If there is a good runout, you can usually let your skis run straight down a chute, but otherwise expect a prolonged session of snowplowing.

Stay low and wide in steep chutes.

Wider chutes give more opportunities to control your speed. Use the terrain to your advantage by skiing up into the sides of the trail, turning, and heading back down and across to the other side to check speed. If you carry enough speed and remain relaxed and square over your skis with your hands out in front, you will find that the walls of the gully will nearly make the turn for you as you bank off their sides.

Ride the sides to check speed.

Moguls: Beaver houses left over after sharp-toothed devastation? No, moguls are the bumpy residue of quick-turning alpine skiers at lift-served areas. You can surely ski them with a parallel technique, staying low in your knees and rolling through the humpy terrain, but tele-marking is another challenge altogether. It takes lots of practice to avoid being choppy, but it's worth it.

In a telemark position, think of being on one long articulating ski, progressing like a rubber boat undulating down whitewater rapids. You have the ultimately flexible ski which can bend like a universal joint, in the middle, to conform to the bumps, actually wrapping around each one. The key is timing, that ability to turn at the right place in the moguls so you don't crash into a mogul wall or clip your ski tails against a neighboring hillock. Do every turn in your head before you get there. Change your lead ski on the top of the big bumps by springing into the air and landing with the front ski over the crest of the bump, then sinking and carving. Smaller bumps require only knee absorption during the lead change. A step telly with a hop is often a quick way to get around. And a double-pole plant helps rapid-fire unweighting. Come down hard on the front part of your ski (on the ball of your foot) to really set your edges and control speed. You must lean forward and commit as if sacrificing yourself to gravity. Work into and around the backside of each mogul, for it is here that you discover soft, forgiving snow, if any is to be found.

Psyching the first turn: Skiing is rhythm. Lose it and you'll feel as awkward as a marathoner in hiking boots. No single turn during a downhill run is more critical than the first, for it determines rhythm, timing, and confidence. Miss it, and the run becomes a series of linked recoveries. Hit it right, and it is the first stroke of a masterful signature on the snowy slope. Good skiers use the first turn to test the feel and consistency of the snow. Here are some ways to get into the first turn:

• Cruise: Tips hanging out over a moderate incline of lovely powder or corn? No problem here. Just start with your normal telemark or parallel but compress a bit more into a stable position for the first turn. This one is usually at slower speed, so you'll need lots of power and definite unweighting to overcome inertia.

- Stem: A stem christie or stem telemark is often the perfect way to pass go and get into the game. It's very secure, with little speed—the better to get your bearings and "read" the snow. No red alert telegraphed from feet? Let 'em roll! Start slow, then let off the brakes. Somehow the old stem, even though it may be brief, feels good at first, like a friend wishing you good luck.

- Traverse: Often the lay of the terrain or pockets of bad snow force you to traverse into the good skiing. Sideslip along the traverse to control speed, finally jamming your heels down at the end to give a firm springboard from which to crank into your first turn. If the good snow lies lower, sideslip over the crud in a steeper traverse, safely losing a bit of vertical. This sideslipping also gives you a chance to plumb the snow, should it be awkward or windswept, without risk, and to plan your attack. You can take your time, looking for the best snow in which to break into the fall line.

- Straight: Hemmed into a narrow chute of trees or rocks for the first few feet? Salivating for that great snow lying below? Try a straight run. Flex those knees. Snatch control by turning solidly as you careen onto the good terrain. To better establish rhythm, try to make your first turn to your strong side.

- Jump: On days of bravado, when air feels good under your skis, jump into a run. Sometimes it's the only practical way to clear rocks or launch from a cornice. Be sure of your landing—that it be forgiving and avalanche safe— and that there is room to garner a measure of control. Brash confidence is needed here, for there is not the luxury to introduce yourself graciously to the work at hand. Look skyward, look earthward, adjust the industrial-strength pampers, and shove off.

Extreme downhills: The day Art Burrows and Ned Gillette climbed to ski the U-Notch was ideal, the snow being slightly wettish as the warmth began to penetrate. The snow was soft enough to edge, yet cohesive enough for a good bond to avoid avalanches. They needed perfection, for the U-Notch, located in the Palisades of California's Sierra Nevada, had never before been skied on three-pin equipment. In the summer it is an ice runnel that attracts climbers. In the winter it is snow filled. It lays at an

Quick lead changes while telemarking in the bumps.

average angle of thirty-eight to forty degrees, increasing to forty-five degrees at the top.

Ned and Art had honed their technique during the previous five weeks of intense backcountry skiing and felt ready for a grand finale to their guerrilla tourism expedition through the West.

"On these extreme slopes, you cannot get stressed out, you must have a certain amount of detachment," Art said at the top, more to himself than to Ned. Extreme cross-country downhill skiing is just as challenging as extreme alpine skiing, but the angle of what is negotiable on three-pin equipment is somewhat less, sometimes lessening the danger factor. In the right snow conditions, almost every slope is skiable on three pins, even the Grand Teton.

Having watched Rick Barker of Ketchum, Idaho, ski the north couloir between Snowpatch and Bugaboo Spires in the Bugaboos, Ned is convinced all you need is experience, strength, and a cool head—not special equipment—to ski well on three pins on the extreme downhills. It's a matter of mind set as much as edge set.

Art ejected into the U-Notch first, delicately edging down the first short headwall. The concrete-hard snow at the top made the angle too steep for a turn on nordic skis. Softer snow would have been forgiving enough, but their boots overhung the narrow skis enough to hit the hard snow and easily could have kicked off their edges. So fine was the margin between too much and too little edge that the usual slight wobbling of ankles in their leather boots had to be totally eliminated through muscle control. Below, the snow softened and the critical angle lessened a few degrees. So did their anxiety. Although still confined in the thin slot, they started turning, heaping one turn instantly upon the completion of the last.

"I'm beginning to enjoy this," Art said slowly. "Ya know, I have the same concentration on each turn when I race. The formula includes no thought of falling. Why worry about the future? It is not now." Ned barely heard him, for the angle was steepening again. He was finally enjoying it too, a splendid mixture of ecstasy, fear and concentration. They were adrenalin junkies, but coldly calculating ones.

This was no place for telemarks, but for the quick initiation and precise edging available from survival parallels. A telemark is a banked, more or less static turn in which instant adjustments are difficult, making it easier to lose your edges on steep, hard pack.

The key was getting through the fall line quickly, controlling acceleration, not getting psyched out by the drastic view down. Each turn was initiated from a stabilizing, decelerating set of the edges, poles planted far down the hill. The total unweighting of the skis to clear the snow was like a subtle jump, a delicate step off into space to rotate the skis one hundred and eighty degrees across the slope.

The lift-off was critical, especially with loose-heeled bindings: an off-balance jump would allow the skis to wave about. The mere swing of the skis into an elevator-shaft

Art Burrows in the U-Notch.

fall line committed the riders to a weightless freedom unknown on moderate slopes. A gravity-aided pivot around the planted pole landed them gently, at nearly a dead stop, facing the other direction, controlled and coiled for the next launch.

Cross-country downhill skis have a light swing weight, so it is easy to position them quickly. When the terrain is extraordinarily steep, the airy change of edges is exquisite. It is like the first plunge of a bird, which is almost immediately controlled by the opening of the wings. To be safe a balanced landing on flexed knees is critical. It is difficult to keep the downhill leg bent, since it is so much lower than the other. The landing must be soft to avoid punching through or fracturing the crust and maybe starting an avalanche. You are actually testing the snow at each turn.

As Ned and Art left the extreme and started out onto the steep fan leading to the glacier below the U-Notch, they dropped into telemarks, but not yet the long radius sweeps where Mach 1 then Mach 2 is achieved with startling suddenness. They still needed control—thus step telemarks: stepping committed into the fall line, coming down hard on the front foot, then bringing the rear ski in close for extreme angulation, before sweeping out on the easy glacier below.

Bushwhacking: Skiing the back country in craggy New England or the Midwest calls for some impromptu and off-beat techniques. They involve plenty of twisting, pivoting, flailing, ducking, lunging, hanging on, and corkscrewing around trees. You won't find these maneuvers discussed here or elsewhere in the literature of skiing. You don't learn *how* to flail on skinny skis, you just *do* it as snow and terrain dictate. For example, when the tight lines of unyielding spruce cramp your style, and your ski poles plunge in to the handles in the tractionless fluff, just let them dangle from wrist straps and pull yourself uphill from tree to tree like a long-toed sloth.

Skiing downhill through trees may become an addictive favorite challenge. Nature's slalom course demands lightning reactions at speed. Pole straps come off the wrists for downhill unless you want to risk the shoulder-wrenching surprise of catching your basket on a branch. In tight trees, you've got to be up on your skis and more than a little cocky. Drive forward even though you cannot see around every corner or over every bump. Protect your eyes by ducking and dodging among the tight branches, arms up, like a boxer. Categories of turns disappear as an upcoming maple calls for a half telemark with a skate turn followed by a jumping parallel conclusion. Call them what you will, but get around the tree.

Anything goes while bushwhacking.

Stream crossing: the anticipation is often worse than the doing.

Crossing streams: Be careful of skiing across rivers or lakes early or late in the season or during thaws, when the ice may be "candled" and rotten. Skis give much support, but a dousing in freezing water is a nasty business.

You can often step across a small open stream if you establish a firm platform and steady yourself with your poles for the forthcoming hop. A more flamboyant but riskier approach calls for a double-pole plant just before the stream and a vigorous spring and vault off the poles. Timing is everything here, and knees must be loose for the landing. Rivers are another story: it's best to test them for depth with a ski pole as you cross. Go barefoot if the river is not too wide or the bed too rocky; otherwise at least remove your socks so they will be dry for further skiing on the other side. Face upstream as you work your way across, and use ski poles as steadying crutches.

Following a two hundred and twenty-mile ski traverse, Ned Gillette and his party descended from the high glacier plateaus of Alaska's St. Elias Range into the lowlands, which spring was already embracing. Conditions deteriorated until they were forced to ski across mud flats and gravel beds and ford rivers recently released from winter ice, all while dragging supply sleds. They never could build up enough speed to water ski, although Steve Darrow tried it, only to have his skis quickly submerge and stick to the muddy bottom, producing a headlong dive into an icy bath! Steve emerged spouting like a wounded whale, wounded in pride only, beaching himself to dry on the sun-warmed shore.

Roped skiing: No matter how safe and free of crevasses you *think* a glacier is, always ski roped up for safety when traveling on glaciers. Compared with foot or snowshoe travel, skis give the added advantage of distributing your weight over a larger supporting surface, thereby reducing your chance of dropping into an unseen crevasse.

Ski with less than half a rope length between yourself and your partner, keeping the excess coiled on both packs. Roped skiing demands close attention to pace, as the stops and starts of one skier are immediately received by the other through the umbilical safety line. This is especially critical on downhills, where a winter Laurel and Hardy act is usually the result of trying to anticipate the next turn. It's easier in front, so put the weaker skier there.

Ski slowly and in control, with the lead skier setting the pace. We've dropped into crevasses up to our waists, but have never had the frightening and sinking feeling of dropping in deeper. As long as your skiing companion is alert and quick in reaction, and the rope is tight, it is possible to arrest a crevasse fall. Once in a crevasse, the situation is extremely serious. The person on top must anchor the rope with ice axes, snow stakes, skis, or even himself. The "spelunker" should be tied in so the backpack can be dumped, hanging on the rope below. Now you are

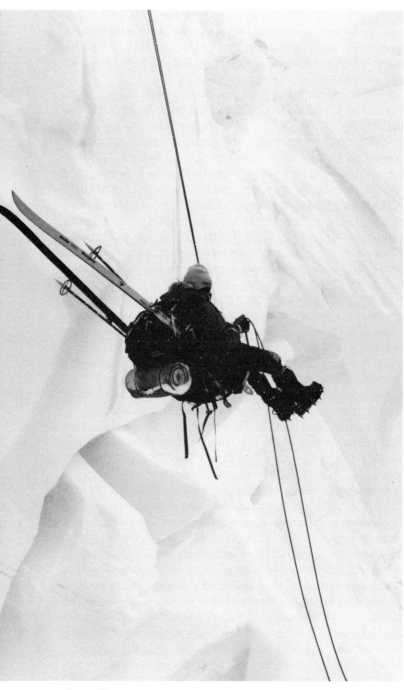

Rappelling.

unburdened, and can work your way up the rope to safety with a system of sliding prusik slings or mechanical ascenders.

While skiing around Mount McKinley in 1978, Ned Gillette had to climb over four technically difficult passes. For safety on the way up his group often set up a secure boot-axe belay in which the belayer's boot reinforces the strength and holding power of the ice axe. This simple belay stance is effective, easy to learn, and fast to arrange. The descents frequently required rappelling down vertical ice cliffs. So you can see that a rope is an invaluable asset for mountain travel, for prevention of accidents, and for self-rescue.

Skier's self-arrest: We've seen skiers resort to a ski pole self-arrest in life-threatening situations. Doug Wiens halted a long slide on the icy headwall of a cirque on Ellesmere Island—he was using three-pin boots and bindings. On their first attempt to climb Mount McKinley in a day, Galen Rowell slowed their fall enough to allow Ned Gillette to grab a fixed rope and stop them. His lightning-quick reactions gave him the opportunity to jam the ski pole tip into the snow up to the basket while gripping the pole with one hand above the basket, the other one higher on the shaft. This technique will probably stop you when nothing else will.

For skiing in extreme conditions, there are specially designed ski poles with a plastic ice-axe-like spike protruding from the handle. And don't be hesitant to change to climbing boots and crampons if you feel insecure on steep, icy terrain.

Coping with Snow

Tracks

Many skiers consider a preset ski track always the same, never changing. But think back: isn't it easier to ski the same track in some snow conditions and harder in others? Just as you might have to change your ski wax each day, so you must change your ski technique to get the most out of the day's conditions, unless you wish to be only a fair-weather and packed-powder skier. With experience, you'll develop an intuitive sense, shifting to the most effective technique.

Harder and faster tracks, such as hard-packed powder snow at twenty degrees Fahrenheit, glazed snow, and icy snow mean faster ground speed and call for some changes in technique. When diagonal striding you can kick harder and get more carry with each stride. But often diagonal striding is not the best technique. You'll get tremendous momentum from double poling and kick double poling, even up some moderate hills. The tracks are unyielding grooves which secure your direction of travel. Since the baskets will not sink too far into the snow you can get lots of push from your poles.

Soft snow requires a very delicate technique. If you stomp down hard on the snow, it will give under your ski, causing you to slip. What you need is a change of technique which is as much a change in feeling. Don't bang uphill as you might on a firm track, but set your ski more subtly with a shorter stride. You need good balance, because the sidewalls of the track are soft and will break down if your ski goes awry. Since the pole track is equally soft, preventing Herculean thrusts of the arms, you'll have to be a little less ambitious with your poling.

Slower snow requires a faster tempo to maintain your speed. Don't hang out on your gliding ski for a long time or your momentum will die. Be quick, get off that gliding ski! If the snow is super slow, use more diagonal striding on the flats. Double poling may be useful only on gradual downhills.

Transitions

Varying snow depth: When skiing down a groomed trail, you often choose to step out into the deeper snow along the edges to slow your speed or are forced out by a trail hazard or fallen skier. This can be an explosive transition as you go abruptly from faster snow to slower snow. You must anticipate this change by sitting back just a little before you enter the powder snow or by dropping into a stable telemark stance.

Varying snow consistency: Sun often raises havoc with snow, changing its consistency in some spots on the trail more than others. Be alert to reading the track ahead so you're ready for the changes. In midwinter the sunny areas are usually faster (powder snow with a *little* more

Track skiing changes with each day's weather conditions.

moisture supplies more lubrication so the skis run faster).
The shady areas are usually slower. However, late winter
and spring conditions usually mean the opposite: the hard
snow and icy areas that are shaded by trees or lie on a
north-exposure slope are faster, while the sunny and
south-facing slopes are slow and sticky. On downhill sections you should be ready to be pitched forward when
entering a slow snow area, and set back on your heels (or
elsewhere) in a fast snow area. Be crafty: look ahead and be
ready for the acceleration or braking action by leaning
forward or sitting back. Which is to say, you take your
chances in a parallel stance; in a telemark, you're stable
whether pitched forward or back.

Sitting back, by the way, preferably with the morning
paper and a cup of coffee, is good strategy for the early
hours of a day with good spring snow. If you venture out too
early you'll be skiing, quite simply, on ice. Better to wait a
couple of hours until the sun softens the snow and conditions are more inviting. At the end of the day snow can
change back from mush to ice with a rapidity that will
rattle your skis. Most types of waxless skis will not work
well in these early and late snow conditions. So for spring
skiing don't champ at the bit and don't push the day's
skiing to its limits.

Icing

Just as the beauty of summer is at times compromised by
the obnoxious mosquito and the tenacious black fly, so is
cross-country skiing often frustrated by peculiar snow
conditions that build up ice on ski bottoms. This usually
occurs at that temperature most dreaded by skiers, thirty-
two degrees Fahrenheit (zero degrees centigrade), when no
wax seems to work, and waxless skis clump up with snow.

Here are a few hints on technique which will help you
ease through these trying times. To prevent the warm air
from warming the ski base, thus making it more prone to
icing, keep your skis pressed on the ground and sliding at
all times; if you stop, move your feet in place.

Late in the winter when the sun is high, or in the Sierra
of California, a new fall of powder snow gets worked over
by the sun very quickly. The top inch or two of snow gets
soggy, yet underneath is dry powder. Great is our woe in the

face of instant icing! The trick for minimizing icing here is to keep your skis deep under the snow where it's consistently cold. Don't pick up your skis and collect surface moisture.

The sun also melts the snow on trees, dripping and causing wet areas beneath. Double-pole through these areas, then continue pressing your skis on the ground after you get back into the dryer snow to sponge off the moisture they picked up.

When skiing through the Brooks Range in 1972, Ned Gillette traveled mostly on frozen rivers. But the rivers were not always completely frozen! Often a thin layer of water—called "overflow"—lurked beneath the surface snow that covered the river. If the skiers were quick enough, they could ski through it, then right on into the super-dry snow of Arctic Alaska, wiping the moisture off on the dry absorbent powder without losing a stride.

Icing can be used to your advantage as well. At zero degrees centigrade, allowing your ski to gather a minimum amount of snow on the base gives secure grip uphill. Usually you'll be able to kick it off at the top. If not, be prepared to walk down the other side!

The easiest way to remove accumulated ice from ski bases without taking off your skis is to scrape one ski back and forth over the other just in front of the binding. Turning the bottom ski on edge gives it a sharper surface for removal of stubborn ice. If you are skiing with someone, have him help by turning his own skis on edge and scraping yours over them. Or scrape over a branch that is lying in the trail, or on an icy patch of snow. Sometimes severely stamping your ski down and back and forth on the trail like an angry bull will loosen ice (and possibly ease frustration). If all else fails, take off your skis and clean them with a metal or plastic scraper or with each other.

Off Track

Skiing through fluff or on a packed avenue is not difficult. It's the stages of snow in between powder and packed that cause the problems. Here your center of balance and the speed you carry are critical. Honing technique to ski it all makes you a complete skier.

Avalanche Gulch runs 6,000 vertical feet down the volcanic cone of northern California's 14,162-foot Mount Shasta. Hard, wind-packed snow, unyielding as macadam, paved the steep upper slopes on the May day that Art Burrows, Rick Barker, and Ned Gillette tackled it. But farther down, the sun had mixed a potpourri of sugar and mush. Top and bottom called for completely different strategies. Without both parallel and telemark expertise, the chance to ski the mountain on three pins would have been lost. You need more than one kind of turn to handle the steep and deep, the crud and trees, the narrow and icy. As terrain, snow, and speed vary, you even need different types of parallels and telemarks.

Todd Eastman, displaying a flamboyant disregard for textbook turns, insists his real learning occurs between head plants in horrific snow while skiing home from work in the dark. As Steve Barnett of Mazama, Washington once said, "Always try every terrain, every snow. Never back off. You'll always learn something, and grin crazily at the bottom."

Ice and Hard Snow

Even with metal-edged cross-country skis, biting into the concrete-hard snow at the top of Avalanche Gulch was extremely difficult. You'll find the same conditions at touring centers on icy klister days with plastic-bottomed track skis. Expect greater than the normal amount of wild sliding and skidding. New skis, with acute right-angle edges not yet worn down, help tremendously. If you have metal edges for true cross-country downhill, sharpen them for better hold. Torsionally stiff boots are essential for control.

On very hard snow, a parallel turn is best, or, as a next resort, a stem christie. Forgo telemarks. Ned Gillette opted for parallel turns on the top of Mount Shasta. It is easier to bite with both skis parallel, easier to get around through the fall line quickly, and, most critical, easier to brake speed with heel checks. The key is exerting a great amount of pressure on that downhill ski—standing on that edge. Dramatic angulation (thrusting your knees into the hill) insures a trusty edge hold. Remember to keep your upper body leaning away from the slope so that your weight is directly over your skis throughout turns. Banked turns lead to quick falls. Many telemaniacs do adapt tellies to firm snow by using lots of angulation, but tellies are not at their best here.

The true telemark is a banked turn with a lot of lean, making it easy to lose your edges on hard pack. If you genuflect, be careful to keep weight on your rear ski so both will carve and hold. A step telemark, which gets you around quickly, is likely to force too much weight onto the front ski. On hard snow, the practical slope angle for effective telemarking is more moderate than in softer conditions. Much speed is gained in the long sweep through the fall line. Art Burrows says, "I ski with my feet closer together in a hard-packed telemark, really a half parallel and half telly. In this way I get more equal pressure on both legs. It's easier to press on the rear ski and get a quicker edge change."

Ski edges grabbing and letting go with staccato chattering? It's due to too much edge. Get on and off your edges more quickly. You'll find skidding is often necessary to slow down on ice. To avoid chattering, edge the ski, less acutely at first but progressively more through the turn. Chattering is a sure sign that either you're leaning too much into the turn (banking) or that your boots are torsionally too flexible, allowing the ski to flutter.

When you get into trouble on hardpack, immediately assume a parallel stance. But in powder, a telemark stance gives stability in tight situations.

Deep Powder

When it comes to powder poaching, cross-country downhill can be just as much fun as alpine. Both parallels and telemarks work, although here the telly, being a steered turn, is truly in its element. You'll have more fun than a gopher in soft dirt.

The first ingredient for handling powder is accepting some speed. Nothing is so hard as a slowly torqued powder turn. Speed allows you to lean into a deep-snow telemark, working against a "bank" of snow. Refusal to sign this contract with gravity is without question the greatest psychological barrier to becoming a powder hound. You have to point them down the hill and let them run, then ride them like a surfer rides a wave. And you have to get used to losing sight of your skis in the deep stuff. The sensation is

Jumping to turn in the thick stuff.

like diving into airy water, and as close to Nirvana as most of us are likely to come.

Maintain rhythm. Think of sliding that front ski forward like the repeated pattern of your diagonal stride. The "set" at the end of one turn is the start of the next. Planting the pole is optional. Breaking this rhythm with long traverses between turns kills timing, most notably the ability to rebound off that set platform to gently rise up and sink into the next turn. When skiing well, you'll find you don't pull out of your rhythm when in trouble but crank into another turn for your recovery. The ability to recover is the key to cross-country downhill. We're all going to fall, but don't give up the vertical without a cat-like gyration of protest, if not prowess.

Establishing one long platform on which the skis are kept evenly weighted will let your skis plane, or float, the easier to turn. Too much weight on a single ski submerges it, destroying your center of balance. Squeeze that rear ski through with a steady pressure to change lead between turns. This will help maintain control by eliminating bobbing up and down and uneven weight transfer. This smooth cruise makes telemarking ideal for toting backpacks on looseheeled equipment.

Parallel turns use the same principles of speed, rhythm, and equal weighting of the skis to establish a strong platform from which to work in powder. Ride a cushion of snow with little edging, but instead of banking into the turns, stay pretty much directly over your skis with your feet together. In the turn, draw your knees up, let your ski tails "stall" down into the snow, then let your tips fall off into the turn. Severe unweighting is called for, but just in your knees; the upper body stays neutral. Rick Barker snorts, "I get low enough so I can smell my feet. I get down like I positioned myself in my surfing days. That centers me over my skis, instituting control. Then I just roll my knees into and out of each turn."

Crud

Most mere mortals don't want to tackle slush, mush, Sierra cement, or mashed potato snow on three-pin equipment. But when nature dumps and you're due out of the backcountry for a Monday morning appearance at the office, read on to pick up techniques of salvage more glorious than carving zorros (the kick turn and traverse of last resort).

We have our ways! As Ned's party dropped lower on Avalanche Gulch on Mount Shasta, they evolved into crudmasters. The cruddier the snow, the more aggressive they became. As always, timing and being centered were the essence of technique.

When the crud is merely extremely heavy powder, you can still steer and ride your skis around in an ordinary telemark. It is a valuable energy-conserving technique, but you've got to customize it to the conditions. It is not such a fluid process as in light powder. Since the snow is dense, once you get your skis turning, they'll "catch" and really whip around. The key is starting the turn. From a definite set at the end of the turn, rise up definitely and unweight during the lead change. Sometimes a double-pole plant helps this launching process; this releases your skis from the grip of gravity and snow to steer into the next turn. Sink and press down and around with great compression in the turn. Don't be afraid to exaggerate the definite rise up and lunge downward (jump on those skis!) to obtain power. Keep lots of weight on the rear ski, then turn with even pressure so you don't sink the front ski and throw yourself off balance.

To ski crud in a parallel, stay low to stabilize yourself. To initiate each turn at this slow speed, thrust your heels down, unweight definitely, then drastically roll your knees into the turn to steer and press the skis around. You can ski this stuff in a parallel, but only through great compression. Feel a lot of twisting in the stomach muscles, almost as if you were throwing the skis in the other direction. Avoid the tendency to initiate each turn by jumping erratically off staccato pole plants. Stem christies are trusty allies here. Even snowplows.

When the snow hardens almost to cement, truly radical unweighting is called for. This means you have to get up and out of the snow to steer around. Telemarking still? Initiate the turn with a step up and around the fall line with the forward ski, thus avoiding the vice-like grip of the mush. Or step all the way through the fall line with two steps by taking the first step with the downhill ski, the next with the uphill, then sink into your telly. Step, step, telly. Count to give yourself rhythm: one, two, three; one, two, three. A low telemark is a strong, stable position for bad snow. It doesn't matter so much what happens to you between stable positions, just get from one stable position to the next. These steps do just that.

You can also simply jump your skis up and out of the snow from one parallel stance one hundred and eighty degrees across the hill to the other direction. Going weightless. Gorilla turns. Terrifically energy consuming. Again, it doesn't matter what happens in the air, only on the landing, a decidedly flexed-knee affair.

Crust and Wind Slab

These are the nastiest of all snow conditions. Crust is usually formed by freezing temperatures after sun or rain; wind slab results from high-velocity winds packing the surface. Underlying both, lurking as in ambush, can be soft snow. Here skiing is stop and go.

During the three hundred-mile traverse of Pakistan's Karakoram Himalaya Ned's party encountered miles of eggshell crust as it dropped to lower elevations on the Baltoro Glacier, skiing beneath what seemed the prows of fifty-foot-high ice ships sailing down the glaciers. They would tiptoe along on top of the crust then crash through into the soft snow beneath. Hundreds of times each day they'd haul themselves, struggling under weighty packs, out of these "holes" with Herculean effort. Even here there are techniques. One man would drop his pack, forging ahead for a couple hundred yards breaking trail. While he backtracked to retrieve his goods, the others hauled their gear along his bashed-out path. Then a new man would plow on, so relaying ahead as a team.

If you're faced with a downhill section, any one of a number of turns might work. One thing is for certain: you'll have to ease into them, skiing with real delicacy and poise so you'll skitter over the crust. If the crust refuses to support your weight, your only alternative is to resort to wild step turns, slow stem christies, step telemarks, or traverses and kick turns, and accept your education as it comes. Slow snowplows often are best. This is no time for bravado. Ice crust can cut shins. Windslab can "dinner plate" away underneath your skis, sending you plummeting.

As you can see in the photos, even Galen Rowell's "milk stool squat" was not up to handling the windblown powder of Kahiltna Pass on the flanks of Mount McKinley, and this playful plunge ended in the surest method of stopping. Fortunately, Mr. Rowell is very durable and seems to be able to survive these flying self-arrests. We wouldn't recommend them for the average ski tourer!

Galen Rowell's unique
method of stopping in
windblown, crusty snow.

Coping with Weather

This chapter is mainly about how to dress for skiing, but it is the *weather* that we are truly concerned with, that dictates what clothing is worn. Let's look into most of the vicissitudes of temperature, moisture, and wind that you'll be likely to meet during your skiing years.

Your aim is to maintain a comfortable body temperature throughout the day's tour. The cross-country skier is in the unique situation of having to deal with both excessive heat gain during the early energetic stages of a tour or race and excessive heat loss during the latter stages when fatigue may be high and weather conditions poor. Wearing correct clothing is as important for the tourist as it is for the racer or mountaineer.

Rule number one: Don't overdress. Until you've seen for yourself just how warm you can get cross-country skiing, take our advice and stay clear of heavy, bulky clothing. It is not uncommon for an instructor, wearing what appears to be little more than a jogging suit on a cold morning, to meet a class that appears to be dressed for an assault on the West Ridge of Everest. This down-filled quilted excess simply will not do. Not only is it hard to ski looking like the Michelin Man, but it's a guarantee of an immediate over-heating of your engine and a sloshing sweat bath.

The secret is to layer so you can tailor your dress to the needs of the moment according to the demands of exertion and weather. Rather than one heavy layer of clothing, you should aim for several layers of lighter items. These different layers trap the warmth your body produces. (Clothing fibers do not insulate; it's the trapped air in and between layers.) Layering enables you to remove a veneer or two to allow heat and moisture to escape. When you rest for an extended period and start to cool down, simply compensate by putting on extra layers. Consider how uncomfortably

There are lots of choices in cross-country clothing — you don't have to be fancy to be comfortable.

you would sleep if you utilized only one great down quilt all year round.

Your clothing should fit your body without pressing or binding in any one place, making it uncomfortable or reducing the blood supply to your extremities. It should be designed to allow freedom of movement. It should be of breathable material so your body moisture can escape but tightly woven so water and snow will roll off and wind will be cut. "Light is right," since insulation is proportional to thickness, not weight. Check that your clothing covers the critical freezing points: head, neck, wrists, waist, ankles. Select ski wear that has flexibility so that different combinations will allow you to dress for touring, racing, multiday tours, and off-season jogging and bicycling.

The watchword is function with style. Good manufacturers first build a suit that has function, then add the style. There is a difference between those *planning* to be in bad weather and those *surprised* by bad weather. Surprised ones are in trouble in poorly designed clothing.

It is not only in bad weather that experienced skiers will carry some extra clothing along or take time to make small adjustments in what they are wearing. Where we live, a popular tour in both early and late season is a four-mile ski up the toll road on Vermont's highest peak. The climb of more than 1,500 vertical feet can be sweaty. So wind shell or warm-up jacket goes on before rounding the last, windy corner. To make the long winding descent comfortable, soaked hat and gloves are replaced with dry ones, or the gloves go over glove liners.

Dressing in anticipation for the kind of tour you'll be on is what matters. Your personal guideline should be to avoid both sweating and feeling chilled. Adjust your clothing immediately at the first sign of either. Sweating can reduce the insulative value of your clothing to ten percent of its original value. Change your clothing as soon as possible after skiing, or at least put on a dry shirt. Chilling can increase your oxygen consumption by fifty percent, and shivering can lead to exhaustion. Exposure to wind sucks heat from the body unbelievably quickly.

For long multiweek expeditions skiers have been going increasingly toward the use of synthetics, which are light, strong, and warm, and dry quickly. On Ned's first expedi-

Dress in anticipation for the kind of tour you will be on.

tion in 1972 he wore mostly wool, down, and a little cotton. Now he wears hardly any natural fiber except occasionally a down parka, wool mitts, and wool socks. (Even the socks are partially nylon.) Maybe the trend will reverse, but the performance of synthetics is very good: fiberpile jackets and mitts, Polarguard or Thinsulate parkas, nylon wind shells, polypropylene underwear, Gore-Tex anorak and wind pants.

The Layers

Transportation: Starting from the inside out, your first layer should keep you dry, allowing sweat to escape and evaporate so you don't feel soaked during or after skiing. There is only one thing that really works: underwear made of polypropylene. It's plastic underwear but with the look and feel of woven cotton—the one piece of clothing on which you should insist. Ned used it for ninety days straight on the Ellesmere Island expedition. Ski racers at all levels favor it, and it has been discovered by road runners and cyclists as well. It is an alternative to nothing because it works like nothing else. Because it's nonabsorbent, moisture is pushed through to the next layer so there is always a dry layer next to your skin. When we did yearly penance at Vermont's sixty-kilometer ski marathon we came in with sweat-soaked hats, shirts, and ski suits but with our polypropylene underwear still dry.

Insulation: Four years ago we wrote that there wasn't much new here, the basic turtleneck still being the standby. But now polypropylene is available in medium-weight underwear, which insulates as well as transports sweat; it may be all you need under your ski suit. Turtlenecks and zipper turtlenecks (good for spring skiing) are now made in polypropylene.

Action: This is the layer that will be on the outside for most of your skiing. It should stretch or be loose enough for free movement and be warm for its light weight. Water resistance is desirable, combined with breathability and some wind protection. This could be a one- or two-piece suit of acrylic nylon, cotton-nylon combination, high-quality poplin, or thin wool (wool insulates even when wet). And polypropylene? Right again. Combined, as a liner, with a windproof outer shell, it's still the material of choice.

Layers allow you to tailor your clothing.

Knickers and knee-length socks or full-length jogging suits are your best bets for your lower body. Socks should be a flat, tight weave of wool or wool and nylon (bulky socks pick up and retain too much snow). Bib knickers are a good compromise between one-piece suits and waist knickers: they are comfortable and eliminate the gap between jacket and knickers. Don't be afraid of investing in a one-piece ski suit; we guarantee you'll feel better and ski better. Many one-piece suits are available in non-flash Clark Kent colors for a less blazing display. Racers and fast exercise skiers will choose slinky, wind-shedding suits in lycra. Somewhat heavier but still form-fitting suits in nylon knits are for those who want more insulation.

Protection: This is your layer of last resort. It keeps the wind and rain out of your insulating layers. Carry this extra insurance tied around your waist or in your rucksack. You have many choices here, the best of which is an anorak, wind parka, or lined warm-up suit big enough to fit outside and over your other layers. Second choices are parkas, vests, and sweaters.

Extreme Cold

During the 1979 bone-freezing pre-Olympic meet in Lake Placid, temperatures dropped to ten below zero Fahrenheit. Most competitors added extra clothing to protect themselves during their all-out efforts. A few toughened racers seemed not to notice the cold, led by a giant bearded Finn named Juha Mieto, who raced the fifteen-kilometer cross-country course with bare hands. Mieto was later one-upped by Russian Nikolai Zimyatov, who not only skied the course without gloves but was said to have done it without underwear as well. Neither option do we recommend for the average touring skier of sound mind.

It was not uncommon during these races to see competitors finish with white hardened patches on cheeks, nose, and earlobes. This is frostnip and should not be ignored. It can be thawed out with the warmth of a hand without tissue damage. A super-cold day at touring centers is an occasion for some frosty socializing as passing skiers alert each other to evident frostnip. Don't shy away from skiing on a crackling cold day. A little extra care in dressing will ensure a pleasant tour.

Starting from the bottom, don't cram extra socks into your shoes for cold weather, as they'll cut off blood circulation. Leave plenty of room to wiggle your toes. Try one of the commercially available lined overboots, designed to let the boot still fit into the binding. Or pull an old wool sock over your ski boot and jam the whole rig into your binding. The sock will ball up with snow but your feet will remain warm.

Overboots for super-warm feet.

Cold feet are a common complaint with many cross-country skiers. Most have probably dressed for skiing long before they've gotten out on the trail so that their socks are already soaked with perspiration. For warmer feet, start out with dry, clean socks.

Wear gaiters (like 1920s spats) for deep-snow plunging. Snow clings to knee socks, then has the unpleasant habit of melting and running into your shoes. Gaiters help prevent soggy socks.

On a cold day fast skiers may be able to get by with gloves. Make sure the glove has extra leather between thumb and forefinger to protect against abrasion from poling. Heavier models are lined with foam, Thinsulate, and, inevitably, polypropylene. Unlined gloves are good for spring and will do double duty when combined with a liner.

Mittens are much warmer. Use wool mitts with a separate outer shell or nylon mitts with a synthetic pile lining. Down mitts are OK if you're training for the Golden Gloves but too bulky for skiing. Still, your hands may get cold now and then. Windmill your arms vigorously in big circles to push the blood into your fingertips. Stay with it for several minutes until your fingers warm up and tingle or until you are airborne.

Speaking of cold hands, it is strangely necessary to turn to noses at the same time. It is not uncommon to see touring skiers take off mittens or gloves in subzero cold to extract a tissue from the inner reaches of their garments. But, once used, the tissue becomes a sodden wad in the pocket or, discarded, a ski-slowing mound in the track. Much better to resort to the St. Nick trick. Lay a finger alongside *your* nose, lean over to clear your skis, and blow through the unweighted nostril. Be assured that in the etiquette of cross-country skiing such a means of discharge is entirely proper.

Your head is the body's most efficient radiator, able to radiate up to seventy-five percent of the total amount of body heat loss. So, the old saying, "When your feet are cold, put on a hat," is really valid. If you're skiing vigorously, a light-weight hat is your best choice. If it's super-cold, two hats are entirely legitimate. Or use a tight-fitting head-band or earband under your regular hat to prevent frostnip of the earlobes. Four years ago it was impossible to get the small, neat earmuffs favored by Scandinavian racers. Now they're stocked by many specialty shops. A balaclava (wool helmet) which covers your entire head except your eyes, nose, and mouth supplies great protection, as does a hand-kerchief tied over the face. Both are good rigs for beginning a life of crime.

Last but not least, a word to the gents. How shall we say this? **Protect your parts!** Groinal frostnip has unfortunately been well documented in medical literature. Some of the companies that make polypropylene underwear offer special briefs with windproof nylon front panels. Lifa's version became known instantly as "fig Lifas." Lacking them, almost anything will do for a Nordic codpiece: a sock, a hat, the *New York Times*, birch bark.... Ladies, ski on! To our knowledge you have no corresponding difficulties.

Head covering calls for imagination.

Wind

The tricks of dressing for extreme cold will protect you from wind as well. For your face you may want to add a hood that is big enough to protect you from a side wind, or a face mask or goggles, so that not even your closest friend will recognize you!

Your chief shield against wind is a good-quality anorak or wind parka. But many garments which profess to be windproof just plain are not. Check them out by blowing through them onto your hand. Is there much resistance? Remember that air is a good insulator as long as it is not moving. So wind-protective garments should keep trapped air next to your body.

Rain and Wet Snow

Avoid getting wet at all costs. It is much more dangerous for you to be wet than to be cold in a dry climate: it's easier to warm yourself up than to dry out, a fact verified by all who ski in the Northwest. Even though the temperature may be above freezing, you can become chilled and helpless in a remarkably short period of time.

A raincoat or cagoule that is totally waterproof is fine to ski in if it is big enough to ventilate from the bottom. Be

Sunny weather is a mixed blessing on expeditions.

careful not to ski so fast that you get a drenching in your own sweat. Better is an outer shell made of Gore-Tex or a similar breathable but waterproof material. Or wear a couple of layers that you feel you can afford to get wet, then change immediately to clothing you have kept dry in a plastic bag in your rucksack. Keep a pair of mittens and socks dry as well.

Heat

Since we usually think of needing protection from cold and driving wind, it sounds strange that we must be careful of serious overexposure to the sun while skiing. In the spring, when the sun is blistering, excess heat can be a major problem, especially at high altitudes, when you can sunburn the roof of your mouth while glacier skiing! It is easy to be deceived about the amount of sun you are getting in the chilled high-mountain air. Discard layers of clothing but consider keeping one light layer on as a sun shield, as the Arabs do. Wear dark glasses, a hat with a sun visor, and plenty of sunscreen applied imaginatively—remember that the sun is reflecting off the snow and can burn earlobes and armpits. Drink plenty of water to prevent dehydration. Sunstroke will incapacitate you just as much as extreme shivering.

Winter Survival

You and two friends are six miles from the road; night is falling; it is snowing. You have been touring all day with some clothing and accessories in your small day pack. And now you have the unsettling suspicion that you're about to become part of a Jack London story.

Apprehension is difficult to deal with as darkness approaches. Keep your head about you and think your next moves through carefully. Stay together and don't be hesitant about spending the night out if reasonable alternatives of escape are slim. Even with a headlamp your chances of getting out safely in the dark are much less than of getting lost and expending valuable energy foolishly. To plunge forward wishfully may only increase your error. You can be quite comfortable if you follow a few simple guidelines. (And you might have avoided the entire situation if you had judged your speed of travel more realistically and turned back while there was still ample light.)

Carefully inventory your personal possessions and analyze how each might help you. Socks don't always go on the feet in a situation like this—they're good mitts as well. Consider using shoestring or belts for rope, skis and poles for building shelter, backpack to stuff your feet into, shoes to sit on, ski tip as a shovel, ski tail to cut snow blocks, ace bandages from a first-aid kit to keep head, feet, or hands warm, and tape as string. Put on any extra clothing as soon as you stop, especially dry socks and a dry layer next to your skin and an outer layer for wind and water protection. Conserve as much heat as possible right from the beginning.

Start looking for a spot to bivouac as soon as possible. Scout out the surrounding area thoroughly in ten to fifteen minutes for the best shelter site: a big boulder for wind protection, a log to crawl under. The conical depression in

Be innovative in finding a shelter.

the snow around an evergreen tree with branches fanning out above is good shelter. Snow is a wonderful insulator, and a shallow trench dug with skis and hands and covered with snow blocks in a V-shaped roof or with tarp held down by skis makes a comfortable little niche in a stormy situation, as long as you've avoided windy ridges and gullies where cold air settles.

If you're caught in exposed terrain as Ned Gillette and his party were during their ski traverse of New Zealand's Southern Alps, dig a snow cave for ultimate protection from ferocious storms. Bring all your gear inside to avoid a snowy treasure hunt after the storm passes. Use a ski pole to keep an air vent open. Gillette's group huddled in relative comfort for one hundred hours, moving on over the glacier when the weather cleared. Travel in this instance was sadly brief—the next day a seven-day storm hit. The four skiers huddled in a two-person tent, wet, miserable and filled with anxiety about the possible collapse of their nylon cocoon. When possible, go underground, young man!

So just settle in like a Neanderthal and make the best of the situation. Remember two bodies huddling together are better than one! Rest assured that plenty of other people have made it through unprotected nights in the winter.

As a postscript, if your companion is injured and unable to travel, the best tack is to make him or her warm, dry, and comfortable (after administering the necessary first aid), and go for help if adequate daylight remains. In the event that you do have to haul an injured skier to safety, it is possible to construct an emergency toboggan out of one or more sets of skis.

In the forest, locate dry tinder, dead wood, or bark for fire starter. The inner lower dead branches of evergreen trees are usually dry even in the worst weather. A big factor in the success of fire starting is an extended search for good wood; take the time while you can still see. A short candle stub will help start the flames. Locate the fire so that snow from overlying branches won't kill it. Build it on a rock if possible to prevent it from melting into the snow, and use a rock, a log, or banked snow as a reflector. You have a choice of building a small, efficient fire to keep warm by or a big bonfire that'll keep you warm running for firewood. Above treeline? Fill your stove before daylight fades.

A couple, benighted on the trail, came in to return two pairs of nicely roasted and charred rental skis, along with melted boots, to the Yosemite Mountaineering School. Although they had built a fire from available forest wood, they confessed to adding their skis from time to time. Normally it's not such a hot idea to burn your means of transportation. Fortunately they left enough of the skis intact so they could ski out the next morning. (Incidentally, you need matches to start fires. If you've forgotten them or they're not waterproof, you'll have plenty of time during the cold night ahead to contemplate your oversight.)

Create a bed or sitting platform from dead branches, meadow grass, backpack, rope, or small foam pad (if you've gone touring prepared) to cut loss of heat via conduction.

Drink plenty of water if available, as it's easy to become dehydrated. Eating snow or icicles will take the dry sticky taste out of your mouth but contribute little toward rehydrating. Eat whatever food you wish that evening if you feel assured you'll get out the next day; you'll need the calories to stay warm during the night.

On the Mount Everest Grand Circle Expedition, Gillette's team did just that near the end of the Nepal segment. They ate the last of their food, not knowing the Sherpas would be unable to reach them with scheduled supplies. The result was a five-day trek out to civilization through deep snow — without food! It was another episode in the high-altitude crash diet program.

What to Carry

The essence of cross-country skiing is moving fast and light. But if you're headed out on a lengthy all-day tour, a few extras are necessary. They can be fitted into a small day pack or distributed among the group.

Quick-energy snacks
Water bottle
Windbreaker
Jacket
Extra socks, mitts, hat
Sunglasses
Sun screen (#15 for maximum protection)
Extra wax
Scraper
Spare tip
Matches
Map
Compass
Simple first aid kit, including adhesive tape for blisters
Repair kit: extra binding bails, Swiss army knife, tiny vice-grip pliers, small posi-drive screwdriver, steel wool, bailing wire, duct or strapping tape, two hose clamps (to splice a broken pole)
High-country kit: stiff plastic shovel, avalanche cord, avalanche beacon, space blanket, small ensolite pad

Yosemite Lesson

On a trip that seems like it happened a century ago, Ned Gillette and his friend Jeff decided to ski the twenty-five miles from Yosemite Valley to Tuolumne Meadows in one day, a gain of 5,000 feet (to 9,000 feet) with lots of undulation in between. They carried moderately heavy packs, planning to stay for a week and do some winter climbing. Starting at daybreak they sped up the steep 3,000-foot climb out of the valley, full of enthusiasm and energy. Donna joined them at the Snowcreek cabin, located at the top of the valley wall. They continued on in fine shape, the goal of making Tuolumne in one day fixed rigidly in their minds. The trail-breaking was difficult but not impossible in typically heavy Sierra snow.

Several miles farther on, at Tenaya Lake, they discovered that they possessed only one quart of water for all of them! (This was their first clue that they should have altered their plans, but it was overlooked in their novice enthusiasm.) They continued on with the sweaty work, now without water, becoming acutely dehydrated. As the sun hit the horizon, they were only about four miles short of their destination. A brief discussion was held about stopping and bivouacking, but with no tent and with the lure of a warm and snug cabin beckoning, they set off again along the unplowed road, just able to find their way as darkness settled at 5:30 p.m.

Ned felt a bit dizzy and fuzzy-headed as they pressed on, now committed to their personal marathon. The snow continued to be difficult to plow through, and their pace slowed. They had overestimated their remaining strength. The final few miles seemed to take forever. At 9 p.m.— sixteen hours after starting—they arrived in Tuolumne, staggering along like mechanical toys at a snail's pace, lurching onto their poles for balance. They were dog-tired, in the initial stages of hypothermia, and desperately in need of water. Stopping at a bridge where the road crossed the river, they could hear water gurgling. Ned took off his skis, grabbed his ice axe, and crawled under the bridge onto the clean ice. Like a madman he beat and hammered the ice in an attempt to break through to the water. Sparks flew, but he was too far gone to heed their message, and it was not until later that he realized that he had been hitting rocks.

Then, as if he'd been shocked by a bolt of lightning, he was alert and in command again. Jeff had just announced that he couldn't feel his toes, and hadn't for a couple of hours. Ned was up on the road, into his skis, and charging across the meadow toward the Park Service cabin. It was locked. Where would they hide a key? Unusually clever, they located it within five minutes, burst in, started the stove, heated water to drink and, alas, to thaw out Jeff's toes, which were waxy white and hard as wood.

Lukewarm water at one hundred and eight degrees Fahrenheit, accompanied by bite-the-bullet pain, brought the feet back to life, but it was obvious that Jeff was a stretcher case and would not ski out, since feet, once thawed, will suffer tissue damage if walked on. (If self-evacuation is absolutely necessary for a limited distance, do it on still-frozen feet for safety.) The cabin telephone still worked, and a rescue was carried out by the Park Service the following day.

Through inexperience, the group never foresaw the repercussions of their risky enterprise and didn't take precautionary steps until the situation was critical (although after realizing they really were in trouble, they did take cool and resolute steps).

You will never eliminate risk. The key in wilderness travel is to precisely calculate your risk. The probability and likely proportions of an accident are thus reduced.

Ned and his companions extended their physical resources to the limit, bringing on extraordinary fatigue, when there was no emergency and a secure bivouac short of their goal was possible. They made themselves vulnerable to committing mistakes of judgment and coordination. Their first mistake was starting out too quickly first thing in the morning, which caused them to perspire freely, losing valuable water and saturating their clothes. They assumed that others had the essential equipment (like water and extra socks) without double-checking. Even though a stove and pot were handy in their packs, they never took the time to stop and brew up. Acute dehydration closed in and appetite was lost as thirst grew, contributing to low blood sugar and slackened energy, which in turn led toward the initial stages of hypothermia.

Jeff wore inflexible mountain boots with cable bindings. Although not always the case, on this occasion lack of the flexing action of an ordinary cross-country shoe caused his feet to freeze, while Donna's and Ned's were OK. The lack of food and water was another major factor in Jeff's susceptibility to frostbite. He didn't tell the others soon enough that he was having foot problems, and they assumed his feet were in the same condition as theirs. Nobody stopped to change to dry socks during the day. (They did thaw Jeff's feet out properly, and although the healing was lengthy, Jeff lost no toes.)

They grossly miscalculated their possible rate of travel as night approached. They were fatigued in body and mind and the last miles were increasingly slow and tortuous. Their goal of getting to the cabin in one day and finishing what they set out to do clouded their reasoning. They paid the price of inflexible thinking and inconvenienced many people in the Park Service.

You don't have to be doing big trips in big mountains to take the proper precautions or to get into trouble. Daily trail sweeps at touring centers often disclose ill-prepared skiers who are lost or overly fatigued even on well-marked trails. The result is usually acute discomfort. But farther out on unpatrolled wilderness trails on a cold January night or rainy March afternoon the stakes are even higher.

More on Hypothermia

The ill-fated ski trip in Yosemite led to the initial stages of hypothermia. The skier shivering at the end of the day in soaked blue jeans and thin wet gloves is headed for hypothermia. If that skier is within easy distance of a touring center or farmhouse, it is not as dangerous as if he had to pass the night in a tent. A friend once skied across the Sierra with two out-of-shape skiers who overextended the first day and were so hypothermic that they couldn't understand simple directions on how to help put up a tent. The wind wasn't blowing, they weren't wet, but they had simply burned all their fuel and gotten cold quickly.

Prolonged exposure to cold (not necessarily below freezing) and wind and wet can cause a lowering of the temperature of the body's core. Heat loss by the body exceeds heat production. If the temperature falls below a certain point (about ninety-two degrees Fahrenheit), the process is irreversible. Symptoms vary with different persons, but the most common are intense shivering, fatigue, numbness, poor coordination, stumbling pace, impaired speech, weak pulse, blue lips, tense muscles, and irrational thought.

You can be very comfortable in snow if you play it smart.

Treat by preventing further loss of body heat, then adding warmth. This means you must find shelter, replace wet clothing with dry and add layers of insulation, get the victim into a prewarmed sleeping bag, build a fire, surround him with warm bodies, and get him into a hot bath if possible. Curiously enough, avoid giving hot drinks to cure acute cases. The body reacts by opening the constricted vessels carrying cold blood in the arms and legs. This flood of frigidity into the body core can be critically negative. Avoid alcohol, which leads to additional heat loss by dilating blood vessels, and tobacco, which reduces circulation in the extremities.

Be careful not to underestimate the extent to which wetness and wind accelerate heat loss. The best way to defend against hypothermia is to avoid the problem by dressing properly and not overextending, rather than treating it once it occurs.

While climbing 23,442-foot Mount Pumori in the Himalaya during the winter, one of the team, thinking the climbing would start momentarily, became nearly hypothermic by not donning a parka at a belay stance. The unexpected long wait, with the skier thinly clad, brought chills. Don't delay. Retain the heat while you can.

High-Altitude Distress

This can be common above 7,000 feet. Headache, nausea, perhaps vomiting, and shortness of breath usually improve after a day or two. Fluids, aspirin, and limited activity are the best treatments.

High-altitude pulmonary edema is caused by gaining elevation too quickly, and is far more serious than mountain sickness. It can happen at elevations of 10,000 feet and above and can be quickly fatal. Edema is most often caused by too-rapid ascent. If you are a ground-grabbing easterner as we are, give yourself a few days before skiing hard in the Rockies. During expeditions to the Himalaya, teams acclimatize up to a month before moving above 20,000 feet for extended periods. Weakness, shortness of breath, and an increasing, rattling cough begin twelve to forty-eight hours after a too-rapid ascent. Blood serum seeps from capillaries into the lung's tiny air sacs. Fluid accumulates, and the victim begins to drown in his own water. The only cure is a quick descent without waiting for weather or medication.

Navigation

As a serious wilderness skier, take a topographic map on all long tours. Learn to visualize the terrain by quick interpretation of the contour lines so you can choose the path of least resistance for travel. Orient the map to line it up with visual landmarks before using it, or use a compass to align the map. Try to keep in your mind a clear idea of the terrain you have recently passed in case of a forced

Use a compass if visual landmarks are poor.

retreat, and a general idea of the distance covered. Roads, rivers, powerlines, and other landmarks that run parallel to your route should be easily located by sharply angling your direction.

Yet no matter how Gillette's party angled their direction at the end of the Tibet half of the Everest Grand Circle Expedition, the trail to the village of Kharta seemed to have vanished. The data on the map, based on the original 1921 British reconnaissance, clearly labelled a path through what was now a vast, bizarre jungle of rhododendrons up to fifteen feet high. After three days of wandering, the party bumped into a band of Tibetan lumbermen. The communications barrier was enormous, but Gillette and associates did get turned in the right direction—one hundred and eighty degrees!—and an eventual meeting with their Chinese liaison.

If you come across ski tracks and wonder which direction the skier has taken, look at the tracks that the pole has left in the snow. Planting the pole usually leaves a tail on the back of the basket imprint as the skier moves forward.

The position of the sun gives a good idea of direction. You can find south by pointing the hour hand of your watch toward the sun; halfway between the hour hand and twelve is south. (Digital watches won't give a very satisfying readout here!) Navigate by the North Star, and remember that in Orion, the uppermost of the three stars in the belt rises due east and sets due west from any point on Earth.

On an earlier expedition, while skiing across the polar ice shelf that protrudes from the north shore of Ellesmere Island at eighty-three degrees north latitude, Ned Gillette's party encountered extreme whiteout conditions caused by the leads opening up in the Arctic Ocean. Visibility was severely reduced. Their normal sense of direction, movement, and balance was lost. There were no landmarks—everything was white, and the compass was not dependable that close to the North Pole. A system of

Ski tracks can show which direction a skier has taken.

Whiteout: where snow and sky are the same.

navigation was finally worked out using the occasional glimpses of the oily sun to orient themselves generally for a certain hour of the day. As the sun moved they adjusted their angle to it. To keep themselves on a straight line of travel when the sun was hidden, the four skiers separated as much as possible while still maintaining visual and voice contact. The last man in line could sight ahead and determine departures to the left or right.

Fog, blizzards, and heavy rain make traveling difficult whatever the surrounding terrain. Featureless terrain adds to your disorientation, and it's best to stay in camp. Not only is it easy to lose your sense of direction and perspective of size, but you just plain cannot distinguish dips, bumps, steepness of slopes or their runout, lips of cliffs, crevasses, or glaciers. Avoid that sinking feeling in whiteout conditions—be overly cautious.

Avalanches

Ned and skiing friends from both coasts took a skiing holiday in Canada's Bugaboos. The north face of Anniversary Peak would be the prize—if they could ski it. It is a magnificently steep bowl, and they craved its powder. But what was the avalanche hazard? The best slopes for skiing in the backcountry are usually those that present the most deadly slide danger: open bowls and couloirs thirty to forty-five degrees steep. The final decision must be coldly calculated, unswayed by the desire of accomplishment, and made after the long climb to the top. Then, they shouldn't be afraid to turn back or change plans if the slope didn't check out safely. Avalanches are the single most dangerous aspect of backcountry skiing.

They had been touring the Bugaboos for the previous ten days, which gave the party a chance to analyze snow conditions. They had punched and probed with their ski poles to get a feel for snow patterns on different slopes. They had made a visual record of surface changes. Rivulets from sun melt on the south-facing slopes vulnerable to spring thaw would be a sign that water might be percolating underneath, lubricating sliding action.

Few snow "cartwheels" had rolled off these slopes. The snow did not sound hollow underneath, and fracture lines were not running. There had been no recent storms with

Avalanches can be exciting from a distance, but at times they are too close for comfort.

new snow falling an inch an hour or accumulating twelve inches or with winds in excess of twenty miles an hour. Any one of these make for extreme avalanche hazard. (Storms starting with low temperatures and dry snow followed by rising temperatures are most likely to cause avalanches. The dry snow forms a poor bond, giving insufficient strength to support the heavier snow deposited later.)

But as they stood at the top of Anniversary's 2,000-foot vertical drop, trackless snow beckoning, they knew that skiers can put a lot of unnatural stress on a snowpack. Most avalanches that cause injury are triggered by the people themselves, their weight being enough to tip a delicate balance. Avalanche prediction is an art, not a science. For every rule there is an exception; experts speak of probabilities rather than certainties. (During the "circumskision" of Mount McKinley, a colossal avalanche, launched by a mountainside a half mile away, dusted Ned's group as they sat eating lunch.)

They also knew that it is impatience as much as igno-
rance that gets people in trouble: shoving off down a run
with a guess and a prayer without taking time to investi-
gate. During the thirty-day traverse of New Zealand's
Southern Alps, even though low on food supplies, Ned's
party had waited three days after a heavy snowfall before
skiing through a narrow valley, because eighty percent of
avalanches occur during or just after a storm. The valley
floor was littered with chunky debris up to ten feet deep.
On the valley walls, every clearing without natural an-
chors had slid.

What fragile layers lay hidden, waiting to slide on Anniversary Peak? Were there rounded hoar crystals down
deep, caused by extreme cold at the beginning of the
winter? Was there a smooth sun crust or rain crust three
feet down, which might grease the intermediary surface?

On the climb to the top, they had been careful not to
traverse back and forth up the bowl, which would expose
them to danger for a long time and might have "cut" a
release. Instead, they found a path along a ridge that
avoided avalanche paths. Although leeward slopes and
cornices tend to be unstable, because of wind deposition,
the small cornice curling out from the summit seemed
secure. The odds say that a north-facing slope is more
dangerous in midwinter, but this was a cloudy day in
spring.

They dug a snow pit with their stiff, plastic shovels and
examined the six feet of snowpack. Art Burrows and Rick
Barker, in the pit, at first felt anxiety. They immediately
saw the layers, but it took time and close scrutiny of individual crystals under a hand lens to determine their rela-
tion to each other. Ned looked at other crystals against his
dark glove, pleased to see they were interlocking and star
shaped. Conclusion: it was a snowpack of strength. It was
safe. They could enjoy it and concentrate on skiing.

Some skiers advise removing ski and pole safety straps
skiing downhill in the backcountry. They did not, wishing
not to lose them in case of a fall. They did zip their parkas
fully up for better insulation if buried under a slide. Turning on their avalanche beacons (tiny radio transmitters by
whose signal rescuers can home in on a buried victim) and
trailing red avalanche cords as backup, they headed down.

During the first tentative turns, they tested the snow before letting themselves really power into the turns. They skied one at a time, exposing only a single member to danger, and were careful to stop at "islands of safety" (clumps of rocks or trees) for protection should the slope let go. They were ninety-nine-percent certain the conditions were bomber safe, but still followed precautions. They watched each other ski so as to pinpoint the spot last seen should a slide occur.

There are two kinds of snow avalanches: loose snow slides, which start at a point and grow in size as they descend; and slab avalanches, which start when a large area of snow fractures and begins to slide at once. Most accidents are caused by slabs.

If one of the group on Anniversary had been unlucky enough to be caught in a slide, he would have discarded all loose equipment, tried to stay on top by a "swimming" action, and worked his way to the side if possible. Before coming to a stop, getting hands in front of his face would have helped make an air pocket.

Before searching, survivors in the little band would have first checked for further slide danger, then marked the place where they last saw the fallen skier. A quick surface search would have been made directly downslope from this point, probing in suspected areas with an inverted ski pole. Avalanche beacons would have been switched onto receive immediately. Having practiced at some length a quick and logical grid-search pattern technique, we would have had a better chance for success than skiers who had not. Fast work is the key, for a buried person has only a fifty percent chance of survival after thirty minutes.

Instead, thirty minutes of exquisite ski plummeting saw the skiers down and safely out onto the glacier below. They were pleased with their calculations and ecstatic to have made the first three-pin descent (the second descent ever) of the lovely, steep bowl they christened the Croissant.

The American Birkebeiner at Cable, Wisconsin.

Citizens' Racing

Citizens' racing is the term used for cross-country competitions that are open to all comers, young and old, fast and slow. The granddaddy of all races is Sweden's eighty-five kilometer Vasaloppet, which annually attracts about 10,000 starters. Olympic-level international competitors line up with Swedes who do no other racing during the year. The local baker may have a bet with his neighbor on who can ski the distance faster. With the clashing of skis and poles, skiers grunting, falling, and shouting, the start approximates a medieval battle. Sheer numbers force some competitors to wait half an hour to move onto the trail. Once on the trail, things smooth out as each person slides into an individual rhythm for multiple hours of kicking and gliding.

In North America our biggest race is the fifty-five kilometer American Birkebeiner at Telemark Lodge, Wisconsin, which attracts some 8,000 skiers. Throughout the United States and Canada there are nearly a dozen other marathons as well as smaller citizens' races during the winter.

The increasing popularity of ski racing in North America shouldn't surprise anyone who reflects on the growth of road races and marathons. Just as a jogger every so often runs under the watch with a bunch of friends, so you might approach casual citizens' racing. That there is more equipment involved, waxes to be tested and applied, and a course that demands more concentration and technique doesn't necessarily make it any more formal or intense. You can be as serious about it as you want to be. We continue skiing citizens' races because they keep us honest and continue to hone our technique. Three to six races each year give us a reason to stay in shape and to throw old racing rivalries into comic relief.

How to Get Started

To get started racing, you don't have to have lots of training, years of skiing experience, or perfect technique. Find out from your local cross-country shop, touring center, ski club, or division of the U.S. Ski Association when the races are being held. Then just head down to the race, wax your skis, and get out there and go for it! (The racing will take care of itself; all you have to do is ski attentively.)

Lots of people get psyched out just by the term *race*. Think of it instead as a long ski and a festive carnival atmosphere with friends you've probably trained with, will race against, and may soon drink beer with!

Your attitude may well determine what kind of a race you have. Get uptight or too intense and you'll not only miss the fun but have poor results. Serious enjoyment is the key to success as a citizen racer. After all, you're probably racing on a day off from work.

Race Strategy

First of all, whatever race you're going to, get there early. Give yourself enough time to get to know the course (this will be your warm-up as well). Sniff around and try to get a feeling first for the more radical sections of the course — corkscrewing downhills, grain elevator uphills, the sudden skate turn. This will also give you a chance to check the consistency of the snow.

If you're skiing very far from your wax kit, better carry a small fanny pack with waxes, cork, and scraper for testing or adjustment. Double-check your equipment: twenty seconds before the start is no time to begin adjusting your pole strap.

Most citizens' races feature a mass start, sometimes much more of a delight for spectators than for the racer who gets caught in the maelstrom. The gun goes off and immediately there is weeping and wailing and moaning and thrashing of skis. How to protect yourself in the midst of this chaos? First stake out your territory in the starting line, placing your poles well to the side to discourage encroachers. Station yourself in the pack according to your ability: if you're a hotshot, get up front; if not, go for a more modest start to prevent being engulfed from the rear. If you can't get up front, you may find that getting to the outside gives you more room to work.

Technically speaking, almost anything goes. Skating across the starting field is sometimes faster, but if the pack is tight you risk instant ski entanglement; double poling would probably be better. Run on your skis if you must — don't let yourself be pushed around, pulled down, or skewered. Go for it in the beginning; the masses will sort themselves out and less frantic rhythms will soon be established, which means you'll have to train yourself to go hard for one or two kilometers to avoid entrapment and then back off the pace.

Keeping a good rhythm going will ensure a good race. Most citizen racers cannot go all out for even ten kilometers. Instead, be clever. Should you be striding on this flat section, or double poling? Can you cruise behind another skier, letting his rhythm smooth out your own and pull you up some hills, or if you've been doing this, is it time to cut

Skiers off the mark at the Norwegian Birkebeiner race.

the cord and make your move? Don't think frantically about speed. Strong, efficient skiing will be fast skiing. Think of speed not as pain, but as getting there easily. If you know the course, push hard before restful downhills.

Along with clever skiing should go clever feeding, especially in longer races. Slow down enough at feeding stations so the liquid goes into your mouth and not elsewhere. Don't neglect the first couple of stations just because you're feeling strong—you'll pay for it later. Don't be bashful about getting enough to drink; you'll probably spill half of it anyway, and only one mouthful of an energy liquid every five kilometers is not going to be very helpful (elite skiers now drink five or six ounces at each station). Nor will the solid food that is occasionally offered. (One competitor in a recent marathon was presented with prime rib at thirty-five kilometers!)

Not all the bumps and dips are in the race course. In a race of any length there are bound to be some highs and lows in your mind. Often in a long race of more than fifty kilometers you will go through several stages when you'll feel you just cannot go on. The worst point in a long race may be somewhere between thirty-five and forty kilometers. Yet these depressions always pass, and concentration and energy will return in the next kilometer. Your body will go farther than you believe it will. And as you push, some highs will displace the lows—a kind of euphoria that seems common to the experience of skiing long races.

Undoubtedly there will be some sections of the course on which you wish you could relax your body as well. Perhaps your wax isn't working very well or the course is especially strenuous. This is the time to concentrate on technique. Slipping on an uphill? Perhaps you're not looking up the hill and have gotten hunched over too far. Feeling slow on the flats? Maybe your poling has gotten sluggish, causing your tempo to drop off. Attention to technique will get your mind off the strain and pain.

Technique

You don't have to ski too many races before you realize that good technique is the key to "free" minutes gained with no more energy expended, especially in races of fifty and sixty kilometers. The super-conditioned racer whose technique is not well developed will begin to thrash and bash during a race, losing ground to a less well-conditioned skier whose technique is refined. Economy of movement that will enable you to ski fast without tiring is your goal.

Since the first edition of this book, interpretation of good racing technique has gone through many changes. We can remember when the talk was of "riding a straight leg," and getting "up on your toes" to double-pole. Indeed, our then model for technique photo sequences has changed his style in the ensuing years.

The catchwords and phrases have been replaced by well-grounded knowledge of fast, efficient skiing, thanks to high-speed film analysis by the U.S. Ski Team and Ski Coaches Association. It all comes down to a few basic components—as true for double poling as for diagonal striding.

Maintaining momentum: This is what all fast skiers have in common, despite personal idiosyncracies of style. They maintain a constant velocity as they ski—arms, legs, and body position all contributing.

How? First, there's no extraneous movement. Nothing to cause extra pressure on the gliding ski that would slow it down. That also means no energy wasted by the skier. And the pressure that must be put on the ski is distributed so that the grip-waxed midsection of the ski won't grab unnecessarily. Finally, poling is begun quickly and with proper mechanical advantage to keep the ski gliding.

Double poling. Not all skiers will get up on their toes as in the first photo.

Double poling: The easiest way to acquire a feeling for these components may be in double poling. If you're compressing over your poles, dropping upper-body weight onto your poles and keeping arms flexed at a constant angle, you're making the right moves for racing or touring.

But some refinements: you will not want to straighten up all the way to recover, but straighten only to a somewhat more forward position. Straight up means more rest but some slowing down because of weighting the ski, and less mechanical advantage in the next pole plant. Further, as you complete the double pole, try to pull weight off the wax pocket of your skis by keeping a fairly straight leg and getting your feet slightly ahead of your hips. You'll feel your ski squirt forward. This is going to be a hard move for those who bend too far over at the waist, nearly putting heads between knees in a wild excess of obeisance. Going beyond horizontal — indeed even going to it — adds no more power and makes you work harder to get back up. Think about initiating not by dropping your head but by dropping or compressing your upper body. Use the stomach muscles!

For maximum glide get feet slightly ahead of knees and hips.

Kick double pole. Left (kicking) foot begins slightly ahead in first photo and doesn't come through until poling begins, third photo.

Kick double pole: Adding a kick to the straight double pole will help you keep up your momentum on slower snow or even slight uphills. The kick comes in as you swing your arms forward. With flexed legs, kick down and back. For maximum thrust, the kicking foot should start a bit ahead of the other foot. You'll feel that your wax will grab a little longer and that you can get a little more purchase this way than if your foot were farther back under your hips.

Now you've opened the scissors, as it were, gliding on one ski, body extended forward, kicking leg extended to the rear—it's that rear leg that acts as a counterbalance so you can get your upper body farther out over your poles. For maximum extension lean forward from the ankles, not the waist.

Begin to close the scissors, but one blade at a time; that is, plant your poles and put pressure on them just as in a double pole. Then begin to bring the trailing leg through. If it comes through too soon, it will inhibit glide and poling power. So, too, will letting your poles get too far out in front. Remember to keep them at a slight backward angle— hands ahead of baskets.

Diagonal stride: Putting appreciation ahead of analysis, U.S. Team coach Mike Gallagher once said that the elite skiers "just seem to float out over their skis." Analysis reveals it's a combination of early, powerful poling, proper body position, and "quiet" skiing free of anything extraneous.

Take the skier stretched out in glide. To keep weight off the wax pocket, he's riding a vertical shin on his front leg — getting a bit of that ski-scooting feel as in the double pole. That will allow him to kick down and sharply with the whole foot while it's right under his body. When monitoring your own skiing, ask yourself where you feel your weight. In your toe (wrong) or in your heel (right)? With weight on the heel it is easier to maintain balance as weight is on the tracking portion of the ski.

Just as the double-poling skier won't absorb and cancel thrust by bending his knees and dropping his rear end, so the striding skier will try to maintain a constant angle of

Diagonal stride.

the knee. Straighten the leg? That only means you'll have to bend it again for a powerful kick. And in bouncing up and down, you disturb your glide and put excessive pressure on the wax pocket of the ski.

To get into the gliding position, a fast skier will not only kick hard but will launch himself forward following a vigorous arm swing. He's not simply reaching forward, a common fault among citizen racers, but driving forward, and letting the rest of his body follow—shoulders, back hips. "Don't leave your behind behind," suggests our friend Lindsay Putnam, a veteran of the U.S. Ski Team. To get it all moving forward, it may help to imagine you're in a body cast from shin to shoulder, moving the whole unit forward. This will be easier if the arm that's poling through continues well past the hip: citizen racers who can't seem to get enough forward drive often are checking the extension of the arm moving to the rear.

A sure sign that a skier is sustaining his glide by poling early is the "separation" between poling arm (left) and recovering arm (right) as the feet are together just before kicking.

If you've brought the whole unit forward, you'll be able to plant your pole early and keep your glide going by getting some thrust from the pole. What you'll do, essentially, is a one-arm double pole. Keep the elbow bent but fused, and use the large muscles of the back and abdomen to supply power.

While this is going on, the trailing leg should still be back. Bring it through too soon and you'll disrupt your glide. Recall the kick double pole: you close the scissors beginning with the front blade—the arm and pole.

Plenty of upper body and a constant angle in elbow for a one-arm double pole.

To kick on uphills compress and roll over ankle.

Uphills: Your basic diagonal stride, with only a few modifications, will get you up hills. You won't get as much glide, so you'll have to increase your tempo and shorten your poling motion. To get maximum glide and bite from your wax, slide the lead foot a bit more forward—as if you're pushing your heel forward. Then compress your ankle, not your knee, and roll over it for best traction.

As much attention ought to be paid to your arms as to your body position. Your arms ought to be crisply driving forward, lifting you up the hill like a high-jumper approaching the bar. There should be plenty of shoulder in your poling to bring your torso forward and give you increased leverage. On uphills, because of the slower speed,

Skiing a steep hill: lead foot slides over knee.

the arm stops near your hip to give maximum push and allow quick recovery to keep up your momentum. How close to the hip depends on how good your wax is and how steep the hill. Bad wax and a killer incline will keep hands more in front. Your arms set your tempo; if they move quickly, your legs will follow. Tired racers pole sluggishly, letting their elbows come out from their bodies, thus losing power. Remember that the arm extension in poling is like a push-up, and push-ups are harder if your hands are way out to the side.

When citizen racers have trouble with hills, it's usually because they straighten up at the bottom and bob up and down rather than try to slide the skis uphill. Or if they tire, they'll hinge forward at the waist and find their skis are suddenly slippery.

Technique for uphill herringboning is much the same in racing and in touring, but you think about it differently while racing. Concentrate on driving the leg straight up the hill instead of to the side. Step way forward each time. Drive your knees forward while your legs and skis are cocked out to the side. Your skis should not be radically Ved out. For quickness you should use as shallow a V as you can get away with. Watch a good skier herringbone the side, and you'll almost think he's diagonal striding. That's because arms are driving forward and there's plenty of

Double pole to get in position for marathon skate.

extension of the rear leg. The upper body is forward: there's no room for bobbing here either.

Marathon skate: Developed by European marathon racers to cover long stretches of flat track, the marathon skate is rapidly gaining popularity, even among citizen racers. If you don't think you need to develop it, try staying with a friend who's skating using only your double pole or kick double pole.

The marathon skate is the one technique, as coach John Estle points out, that could not have been developed without modern tracksetting, because the tail of the skating ski is laid over the tail of the ski remaining in the track; but because of the deeper machine-set tracks, the skis don't touch, and the skating ski can bite into the hardpacked snow along side the track.

Lift the skating ski and splay it to the side as you begin to double-pole. When you double-pole here, you'll want to flex your knees. It compromises the power of the double pole, but flexed legs are what give you the power to skate. As the double pole nears completion, skate out to the side.

If you aren't getting much thrust in skating—the muscular demands are considerable—it may be because you're not compressing enough and are trying to skate off a straight leg. Or you may not be progressively angling the edge of the ski into the snow during the leg extension. Off balance? You may be skating from too low a position, or you simply may not have spent enough time getting comfortable with the maneuver.

Tempo and Terrain

Seasoned racers continuously use terrain to their advantage. For skiing in slow snow and difficult terrain, use a quicker tempo to maintain momentum. When you're skiing uphill on tracks that are filling in with soft snow that is shearing away from the hard track underneath it, you may have to adjust the kind of pressure you put on your skis, going up "on little cat feet." It's the same kind of adjustment you'd make when running on a snowy road. If an uphill track seems slippery, you might get better traction on the packed snow off to one side.

Which is to say, be an opportunist. For example, don't get stuck in the trough between a downhill and an uphill, but take some short, quick double poles to carry your speed as far up the other side as you can, then use quick hands in diagonal striding to scamper up the rest of the way. Perhaps you can switch tracks and cut corners. Or skate over the top of a hill. The better you handle transitional terrain, the better you'll keep up your momentum.

Making the most of changing terrain. Left arm stays forward (second photo) so the right can catch up to it (third photo) for the kick double pole off the top of a hill.

Training

You'll feel better racing in February if you've done some training in September or earlier. Again, training doesn't have to be super-serious business. If you're getting into citizens' racing, you're probably already a jogger or road runner, cyclist or hiker. The thing to do is to build on your already developed cardiovascular fitness while adding some specificity; that is, activities that most closely resemble skiing movements.

Why be specific? If you start skiing in early November having spent the summer running, you'll quickly find the small of your back and abdominal muscles strained and throbbing and your arms devastated. Clearly some upper-body work should have been introduced into your training by early fall. It's by now a commonplace of sports physiology that the best training activities for a sport are those which most closely simulate the movements of that sport.

While running gives a strong foundation of fitness, some modifications are necessary. Vigorous uphill hiking, driv-

Ski striding with poles builds strength and simulates skiing.

ing the foot forward and extending the rear foot behind, coupled with an aggressive arm swing is a better approximation of the demands you'll put on muscles when you ski. Add your poles to this and the effect will be even better. Not only will you strengthen your arms, but with a little concentration and coaching from a friend you can eliminate technical errors as well, such as levering your elbow back instead of driving your hand down and back past your hip. Take your ski poles on a hike, using them on unbroken uphills.

You'll see an increasing number of people out on the road on roller skis. Roller skiing is not for everyone. They are expensive to buy (around $160) and maintain, as tires can wear. Since there are no tracks, your diagonal stride must be well grooved. And you must be careful to ski on roller skis as you would on snow skis: it's very easy to develop a late languid kick because of the ratcheted wheels, rather than the quick, downward punch needed to set your wax. Sharp carbide steel tips on ski poles are vital. To keep them sharp, we've found that an inexpensive sharpener with diamond particles works best.

Whether you're patrolling the roads on roller skis or hiking with ski poles, incorporate variety into your training: one long-distance workout for endurance, perhaps twice as far as you normally race; some intermittent speed work, like running the hills hard with your poles, then letting up on the flats. Races are won on the hills, so plenty of vertical should be included. To get used to racing speeds and to the demands they put on the body, roller skiers will ski a loop of, say, ten kilometers weekly, trying to ski slightly faster each time.

Skiing demands strong back, stomach, and arm muscles. Back lifts, sit-ups, pulling arm bands or Exer-genie, and working on a roller board are all effective. Do your exercises no more than three times a week in sets of ten and gradually add resistance. Through repetitive sets you build up your mind's ability to handle stress and your muscles' ability to keep working after they are tired. Strength work is especially important for women since they usually have not been encouraged to develop large muscle groups.

Remember through all of this not to burn yourself out by pushing too hard or by being obsessive. Listen to your body tell you what it needs and when to rest.

Roller skiing simulates snow skiing.

Ruth Glacier on Mt. McKinley.

Adventure Skiing with Ned Gillette

In contrast to most mountaineering expeditions, which work out of and consequently are tied to one base camp and one location, expeditions using light cross-country skis allow one to rummage through some of the most magnificent terrain on earth, always on the go like mountain gypsies.

Adventure skiing, for me, has meant traversing the three-hundred-mile length of Pakistan's Karakoram Himalaya, telemarking in Tibet, and skiing from the summit of one of China's highest peaks. It has meant five hundred miles of self-sufficient sledging near the North Pole, skiing around Mount McKinley, then pulling off the first one-day ascent of North America's highest peak. It has meant heli-skiing in New Zealand and powder poaching in Canada's Bugaboos. Adventure skiing has also included coaching young Chinese athletes at the invitation of the Chinese Sports Federation in Heilungkiang Province.

Much to my surprise, I have found that adventure skiing, even though outlandish, has opened unexpected doors. It has given access to relatively forbidden areas of the world, like the far west of China, and to fascinating people and exotic cultures.

Meanwhile, Back Home

Skiing has not always been so exotic for me, though — and chances are not for you either. But you don't have to travel thousands of miles or spend a lot of time or money for adventure. With a little imagination and research, it is possible to head off the beaten track and on your own in Canada and the United States. Though I was brought up in

Vermont, my first twenty years of skiing were limited to alpine lift yo-yoing (which I still thoroughly enjoy) and cross-country racing. I never considered using skis as tools of transportation. Following several years in the West and several long ski expeditions, I returned to Vermont and discovered a whole new world of off-track skiing in my own backyard.

Although long treks have their magic, I often as not reap the most satisfaction from day trips close to home. From a one-day skiing trip along the whole of New Hampshire's Presidential Range, I particularly recall a bobsled-like, rocketing run down a tree-shrouded hiking trail deep in powder, always playfully flirting with disaster. I felt gravity-squirted, like a watermelon seed pinched between finger tips. Even closer to home, after a long writing stint in my study, I enjoy touring from the back door to my neighbor's sugarbush and blasting down through the stately maples with an enthusiastic abandon unknown to me at the typewriter!

After relentless track training, it's not unusual for racers to get itchy and spring into the trees and fire off a couple of tellies in space available. Indeed, it's healthy.

As You Like It

All of which leads to the definition of adventure skiing as moving off the beaten track on your own terms. Each person is an adventurer in his own right. Skis are the perfect tools for snowy exploits: the means to discover not only winter but a freedom outside the normal bounds of society, where self-reliance is a happy challenge. Adventure skiing brings back the origins of skiing: setting off across the landscape without paying, without crowds, without dictated fashion. How many times have you skied the tracks at your local ski area? How many times have you cavorted in the trees and unbroken snow to one side of them? We're not talking headwalls or cold sweat, just a change for the better. Jump.

Supple Skiing

So now you know the ancestry of those merrily unmanicured snow signatures beyond the marked trails; a skier has been unabashedly bitten by his pioneering heritage. A

Fresh powder on the Teardrop Trail, Vermont.

perfectly professional instructor has genuflected onto powder on a wide curve off the machine-set tracks and returned to kick and glide, leaving a single, skinny telly track of spontaneous inspiration. The sport is changing. Track skiers are out in the woods and bowls where uniqueness spells quality. Here, every vertical foot to swoosh down is valued, not to be squandered as at a commercial lift area. Off-trail skiing somehow develops a comradery of working with friends, not outdoing them, and a goofy kind of fun as you solve the unexpected problems of cranky snows or tight-treed gullies or a forgotten corkscrew for the wine.

The beauty of this unpolished experience is that it can be done anywhere there is snow. It is the essential ingredient of the suppleness of skiing. If some days the preset tracks of a touring center are icy or rutty, head off the track to save the day. Being a backcountry skier also allows you to extend your season. When commercial areas shut down in the East or the Midwest is out of snow, you'll still find great skiing on eastern ridge tops or in the Rockies, Cascades, and High Sierra far into April, May, and June.

On the flats in front of Mt. McKinley.

Sweet and Sour

Off-track day tours, overnights, alpine touring, ski mountaineering, expeditions: all offer more variability of terrain, snow conditions, and weather than lift-assisted or touring center skiing (though these practice slopes and commercial ski trails can be stepping stones of confidence from which to move into the mountains). Steep icy head-walls of ancient cirques test the skier's mettle, as do breakable crust and deep powder. Pulling across a vast, snow-covered plain into the biting teeth of a brisk north-erly with no sheltering rock or tree in sight demands the resolution of the marathon runner. The onslaught of dark-ness with three hours of traveling still ahead demands an experienced mind to control a wild imagination and a fatigued body.

These journeys into a frozen land, deep in hibernation, are at times frustrating, tedious, grueling, cold, and seem-ingly too much trouble. You are unrealistic if you think you'll always avoid cold, unworkable hands and the trauma of breaking trail in heavy, soggy, cement-like snow. It is all to be expected. Accepted. And it can be horribly exasperating in its fickleness. But then the sun comes out, or that long-sought-after bowl of sheltered powder is cut with your telemark alone, or the stove finally heats the tea water, or you're laughing over that same ridiculous joke with your mates. People are adventurous in direct proportion to the shortness of their memories. Our selective memories always draw us back for more of the reality of being out on our own—committed, self-sufficient, curiously and simply challenged.

How To Get Started

Guide services: Whether or not you sought instruction in the basic techniques of skiing, I am most emphatic recommending a good guide service to adapt your skills to the backcountry. Most mountainous areas in the United States and Canada support outdoor schools, which teach rock climbing in the summer and mountain skiing in the winter, plus survival. Remember that potential danger is far higher in true backcountry skiing than in ordinary skiing. The information garnered from a knowledgeable guide increases your odds of safety, not just your number of pretty turns. Solid information, followed by experience, is your first building block toward competent skiing in rugged country.

Day tours: Start by doing day tours or just hour-long stints off marked trails. Many touring centers have trails that are ungroomed and unpatrolled. Day tours aim for the most exquisite skiing. They allow you to choose the weather and snow conditions you prefer, whereas during multiday treks you are often forced to travel in storms or unruly snow, which raises the level of commitment and potential for error. Plan your itinerary so the length of the tour can be easily shortened if necessary, and consider following unplowed roads to insure gradual grades and foolproof navigation. Day tours present less risk by staying closer to civilization. Finally, the small, light-weight packs used on day tours give more freedom of movement than those required for long trips. Short jaunts allow you to play and try new things.

Mechanical help: Gaining the vertical, moving up to the high ridges, is a key problem. I rather enjoy the steady rhythm of skinning uphill. But for many, the fun of a day tour is often submerged under the sweaty ordeal of busting trail upward. Be clever. Consider driving to the top of a pass served by road, maybe shuttling autos for more runs. Or ride the lifts at a commercial alpine area and ski out onto undeveloped terrain from the summit terminal. Make certain you check with the ski patrol on the policy of skiing out-of-bounds (some areas never allow this type of skiing). Also check on that day's avalanche danger: when there is no danger of avalanche, most western ski areas open the backcountry served by their lifts. Or consider travelling the tracks of touring centers to move quickly to the backcountry.

Possibly a high altitude record for camel carriers: to 17,000 ft on the way to Mustagata in China.

Guidelines for the Outback

Over the years I've developed a few guidelines which help ensure the success of my expeditions. They're applicable to your tours as well, regardless of their length in days or miles.

Self-sufficiency: This is the overriding precept of any expedition or tour. It is a way of organizing your itinerary and gear, but it is also a state of mind. It is often not the number of resources that provides the key to escape from a tight situation but exactly the right ones used in an innovative manner. During the Karakoram Ski Traverse Expedition, vinyl duffle bags became sleds when lashed to thick, pliable plastic sheets. In this way we avoided shouldering all of our allotment of one hundred and twenty pounds per man in backpacks. On another expedition, stormbound with burned-out flashlights in a snow cave in New Zealand, medical gauze stuffed into a canister of hard ski wax became a candle. Even on short day tours, a lost binding bail can prove disastrous. Bring essential repair and survival gear. Expect the unexpected. Be self-reliant within the team.

Limit dependence on the outside world and on the fickleness of nature. For the High Arctic Expedition on Ellesmere Island, we elected to haul two hundred and forty-pound sleds over the polar landscape in order to avoid the questionable dependability of bush pilots to resupply us or of preset food caches, which might be destroyed. We were truly self-sufficient.

Keep your trips exquisite in their simplicity. Every aspect of the endeavor, whether it is food, equipment, size of the team, or choice of route, should be reduced to its lowest common denominator, thus lessening the number of things that can go wrong.

Risk: As your ski trips get longer and more committing, you will find yourself adopting a wary attitude toward flamboyant playfulness on skis or chancy solutions to route-finding problems. A dislocated shoulder, from Grand Prix speed, or equipment lost in a river crossing takes on grave importance in proportion to the distance from rescue. Ski well within your ability; don't ski at your limit unless absolutely essential. Throwing the dice is seldom worth the potential loss. Calculate your risk precisely. The first mistake often starts a chain reaction, quickly turning the trek into a rescue mission. To avoid foolish errors, I always concentrate on finishing one operation before starting the next. On the other hand, you cannot attack the wilderness tentatively. What you are after is a steady strength of judgment and spirit. And, once in a while, even on the riskiest expedition, you just must let go and play to recharge, as we did in Tibet: jumping cornices under the flanks of Everest.

The general rule of thumb in the mountains is to never totally extend and commit yourself unless the goal justifies the risk (which it seldom does). However, once in a great while you choose to go for it, and with luck and careful calculation based on experience, extreme accomplishments far beyond normal limits have a chance of success.

In June 1978, Galen Rowell had the idea that Mount McKinley could be climbed in a day from 10,000-foot Kahiltna Pass if everything went right—us, the snowpack on the trail, and the weather. McKinley had never before been approached in this way. It was a long shot, but he had it exactly calculated. I agreed to go along. After a climb more exhausting than we thought possible, we stood on the 20,320-foot summit on one of those rare still days of brilliant sunshine at the top of North America. Without the gift of perfect weather, either the climb would have been aborted at the lower elevations or I would not be writing this book today.

Team size: I believe in keeping ski expeditions small—no more than four. Four is small enough to provide a cohesive, single-minded unit in keeping with the simplicity of going to the mountains. Additional members increase possibility of error or injury as you move through great chunks of landscape far from the nearest village. Even if you're not going far afield, always make certain your group size is manageable for the itinerary planned. How fast the band can move is the primary margin of safety. Along most extended routes there are dangerous areas across which you must go as quickly as possible. While circling Mount McKinley we had no alternative but to rappel from Traleika Divide, a steep 1,500-foot slope with a southern exposure underlain by ice. The sun roasted the route, and we were giddy with apprehension that the

Making tracks in the Karakoram.

entire slope might slide. But with a small, light team, we got on with it early in the morning and got off it quickly.

Team members: First, you'll want everyone competent in the technical skills demanded—skiing, climbing, rope work, avalanche reading, and so on. When situations are critical, you don't want people who have to figure out what to do. Action and reaction must be second nature. Familiarity breeds out risk.

Second, you'll want strong-willed individuals who nevertheless can work for the common good. Conflict does not spring from these strong wills, rather from a too inflexible view of the intinerary or goal. Remember what your ultimate goal is: having a good time outside with good friends—an adventurous holiday, if you will.

Third, determine everyone's expectations. Does one want to photograph primarily while the other two want to press forward and make miles? Different goals create friction, hamstringing the competence of a party. Plan a strategy before the trip and pick people who are going the same direction.

Fourth, know the people you are traveling with, both their strong and their weak points. You may have to depend on each other rather unexpectedly, as Galen Rowell and I did during our abortive first attempt to climb Mount McKinley in one day. Our rocketing fall, roped together, was arrested by a desperate grasp for an old fixed rope left by previous climbers. Six more feet and we would have slid over the ice cliff. Galen's face was badly cut and bleeding profusely; he went immediately into shock. We were totally tangled and precariously balanced on the tip of disaster, so that one false move by either of us would have ended it all. Galen functioned magnificently, and the retreat, although painful, was without further incident (except for my tumble into a crevasse).

Leadership: The best leadership comes from the team as a whole, individuals taking mutual responsibility for each other. But you still need a leader on any trip, even if everyone is an acknowledged expert. I like a leader who gives the picture of ruling by democracy but who in truth is ruling by benign autocracy while making sure that everyone is assured recognition.

Mt. St. Elias, Alaska.

Eve Ice Fall, New Zealand Alps.

Research: Plan your trip carefully. Know the lay of the land, the snow conditions, and the weather you'll most likely encounter. A young man left Yosemite to take a solo trip of fifty miles into the backcountry. Since it was April, he took only klister wax. A storm dumped three feet of new snow when he got to the higher elevations. He had no way of removing the klister. Fortunately he was better prepared physically than otherwise, and by brute strength he clomped the last twenty miles in knee-deep snow, with three inches of ice clogged on his ski bottoms. All this could have been avoided by prior planning.

Equipment: Choose equipment that won't self-destruct under constant demand and will perform to a standard to ensure safe negotiation of an icy chute or closeknit trees. Just because you are in the mountains, don't assume you must use heavy, ponderous gear. With today's methods of designing fiberglass skis, strength can be attained without sacrificing lightness. After careful research, we decided that we could get away with forty-seven-millimeter-wide skis and light three-pin boots and bindings to ski 1,250 kilometers across Ellesmere Island. These light skis provided the speed we required over a route chosen to avoid the harshest terrain. They also enabled us to do some of the finest downhill skiing I've ever encountered.

In circling Mount McKinley, we even used fifty-millimeter racing boots. Honestly, though, it was just to prove the point that the new racing gear was strong enough for such use. We've since gone back to metal-edged skis and heavier three-pin boots.

Conditioning

Many people are curious to know what kind of conditioning I do for demanding multiweek mountaineering expeditions. I keep myself in generally good shape, but concentrate on honing the specific muscle groups of whatever discipline the upcoming expedition entails: skiing, technical climbing, kayaking, and so on. No matter how strong you are, an eighty-pound pack is always terribly heavy! Further, if the expedition is of two to three months duration, you'll want to start in less than tip-top shape so you'll peak for the "summit"—just as you'd want to for your most important citizens' races late in the season. Remember, it is your mental freshness that is always the key element.

The late Doug Wiens, who shared many expeditions with me, had his own proven method of "training":

"It is obvious that ski expeditions are energy-demanding; what is not so obvious is how to train in order to have the most energy available when it is needed. The accepted method has been 'working-out': running, roller skiing, weights, Exer-genies, and other such futile exercise. These exercises demand energy which I feel is squandered. Before an expedition you shouldn't waste energy, you should save it and store it; hence I've developed a method I call Horizontal Training. The basic rule is, Never stand when you can sit, never sit when you can lie. With proper storage you will accumulate vast energy reserves which can burst forth for explosive and extended effort.

"Some have confused this with mere laziness—not true. This is an exacting training schedule which demands long-term commitment and discipline. Nine to ten hours of sleep are a must, especially sleeping through till late morning to avoid this energy-draining time. Frequent siestas are also beneficial. A unique diet is important so the energy can be efficiently stored and not leak out. The combination of beer and pizza has been found by much experimentation to contain the proper balance of nutrients to maximize the storage of energy! Bon appetit and good training!"

Winter Photography

No matter if you're making a serious expedition or doing some day touring with friends, someone in the party will doubtless have a camera along. Winter photography is not quite as easy as summer shooting, so I'll offer a few hints to help you avoid some of the errors I made while learning how to record the events on expeditions.

On our 1978 ski around Mount McKinley, four photographers took 9,000 transparencies in a three-week period and brought back some great photographs. (We did more skiing and climbing than photographing although it doesn't sound like it.) National Geographic ended up using only eight in their magazine! You've got to shoot a lot to get good. I am purely a point-and-shoot man, proof that anyone who sets mind to it can become proficient.

You must be willing to work for good photos. Try to get different camera angles on your subject by lying on your stomach and shooting up, or hiking up a nearby hill and shooting down. Use your imagination! Don't be afraid to set up the scene. Vary your shots further by using different lenses. On expeditions when I'm severely limited by weight considerations I use a twenty-eight millimeter and an eighty to two hundred millimeter zoom as my standard lenses, each on a separate body. Two bodies are good insurance, plus you don't have to keep changing lenses in snowstorms.

Have your camera ready for use. That white-tail deer isn't going to wait around while you wrestle your camera out of your backpack. Keeping your camera around your neck on one of the many special tight-fitting harnesses is the quickest. Since I dislike having my camera knocking about, I wear a fanny pack backwards, which gives me reasonably fast access to my cameras. With this system I can still tote a backpack. Keep your camera shutter cocked

Jan Reynolds in Eve Ice Fall, New Zealand Alps.

at all times. Don't worry about the occasional wasted frame from accidentally tripping the release. Be ready to capture that once-in-a-lifetime shot.

Most people bring home only photographs of the majestic landscape on a grand scale. These shots are easy; they just beg to be taken. I try to concentrate on close-up shots of what the people around me are going through on the trip—reactions to fatigue, danger, humor, bad wax, nasty weather, and each other. Portray the human reaction to the environment. The photos that usually bring the house down during my adventure slide shows are rapid recording of the circumstances that brought the skier down: Galen's wildly processional, gravity-defying abandonment of anything that passes for downhill control on the McKinley expedition.

Exposure is tricky in the snow. You can pretty much trust your meter for the wide panorama shots. But if it's the person in your frame for which you want to expose correctly, you must be more clever. Get your reading by holding your meter up close to your subject's face, or take a reading off your own hand. As a general rule, if you're shooting people, an exposure of f/5.6 at 1/500 second with ASA 25 film is always close in bright sunlight on snow. Bracketing, or taking pictures at one f/stop above and below the meter reading, is a good idea for important shots. Remember that the colors are richer and shadows longer early and late in the day. This is the time for those dramatic pictures. Midday light is deceptively flat. Cloudy days are fine for portraits.

Moderate cold by itself does not harm equipment. Condensation on camera and lenses will be a problem only if you are constantly warming and cooling a camera: walking inside suddenly to a warm room, or placing the camera next to your body then out in the cold for long periods. You have to make a decision to keep your camera either body temperature or outside temperature on multiday ski trips. I choose to keep my Nikons cold and my small Rollei 35 warm in my pocket.

Cold hands are troublesome in winter shooting. With a lot of outdoor work, it is possible to toughen your hands somewhat so you can handle your cameras for long periods without gloves. Silk inner gloves are a good compromise. And you *can* get proficient enough with mittens to work a camera while keeping your hands toasty warm.

Equipment

We all know what is supposed to happen when a certain number of monkeys gets unlimited access to a certain number of typewriters. Over the years, we and our friends have somehow had access to equipment from major manufacturers and have skied on this gear in our characteristically intense, playful, but analytical fashion. What you get is not Shakespeare but some pretty strong opinions—and some resident confusion—on cross-country gear. It is astonishing how long it takes even experienced skiers to evaluate equipment and find the gear that best enhances their style and level of skiing.

If we were to go into equipment thoroughly enough to satisfy the inquisitive eagle-eyed technician, this book would have been delayed a year, and by now the chapter would be obsolete anyway. The best thing we can do is give

Choose gear that is suitable for the type of skiing you do most frequently.

you some suggestions on how to nose out good equipment. Most important, be willing to bend the ear (and flex the ski) of an experienced cross-country ski instructor in an expansive mood. We cannot emphasize this strongly enough: it is only by practical on-snow experience with equipment that you'll find what is right for you. Season after season we're reminded that cheap, poorly designed equipment can make skiing quite frankly unpleasant. Which is to say, don't buy cheap. If you are a cross-country skier, you're probably also a runner. Or a hiker. Maybe a tennis player. Do you pursue these sports in $10 chainstore shoes? How long would you stick with tennis, outfitted with a $25, prestrung racket?

Cross-country gear is often marketed in packages — skis, boots, and poles priced collectively. There are some legitimate values here, but beware the $69 special. The hook in package deals is usually an attractive ski. But the quality of boots, bindings, and poles making up the rest of the package can be dubious.

Many folks want one ski or boot that will be suitable for racing as well as mountaineering. This simply isn't possible. If you can afford only one set, get what is appropriate for the kind of skiing in which you plan to participate most often. In all probability you'll find the sport enjoyable enough to buy a second, more specialized, pair later in your career.

If you do most of your skiing in prepared tracks at a park or touring center and are an athletic skier, you might go for racing equipment or high-performance, light, touring equipment. But that gear is less suitable if your kind of skiing is over the river and through the woods on ungroomed snow; wider skis with somewhat stiffer tips would be the choice.

Skis

Bases—waxable or waxless: Your first decision must be whether to go waxable or waxless. You can eliminate half the skis on the market by deciding whether you want the performance and adaptability of a waxable ski or the convenience of a waxless ski. A waxless ski will seldom outperform a well-waxed ski, but it will always outperform a poorly waxed ski. Two-wax systems do simplify waxing, but if you view waxing as a hassle, don't hesitate to go waxless. Keep things in perspective: it's more important to be out there skiing than to be skiing on any particular type of ski.

The following information concentrates chiefly on the pros and cons of waxless skis, not because we're pushing you in that direction (quite the contrary, actually) but because we think you need a thorough understanding of the waxless concept before making a decision on which way to go. There is no better feeling in the world than speeding down a well-prepared trail on skis that are perfectly waxed. A waxless ski will never provide that feeling. You just have to determine if performance is worth learning how to wax. For us it certainly has been. With this, let's move on to waxless skis, but be assured that more on waxable skis will be found in the chapter on waxing.

We think fifty percent of the skiers in this country ought to be using waxless skis, but we also think everyone ought to know what is gained or lost by going waxless. Mike Brady, who brought a lot of the European knowledge of cross-country skiing to this country, states the case this way: "When waxable skis are easy to wax—say, in powder or spring snow—waxless skis have no advantage. Only when it's difficult to wax skis, such as in transition conditions (freezing point), do waxless skis have any measurable advantage." Waxless skis have been used successfully in international racing to overcome difficult waxing problems. Bill Koch had the third fastest leg in the 1976 Olympic relay, and Norway's Per Knut Aaland won a silver medal in the 1979 Holmenkollen fifty kilometer. For the last two winters, U.S. Ski Team members have been creating instant waxless skis for difficult waxing conditions by roughening the midsection of their skis with coarse abraders. They call the ski "hairies," and have been trashing the competition.

Although many waxless skis are effective in certain conditions, don't expect miracles from them. Their base designs offer only one solution for the variety of snow conditions you will meet out on the trail. As Harold Bjerke of Swix Sport International (a major wax manufacturer) says, "Just remember that using a waxless ski is like playing eighteen holes of golf with only the putter."

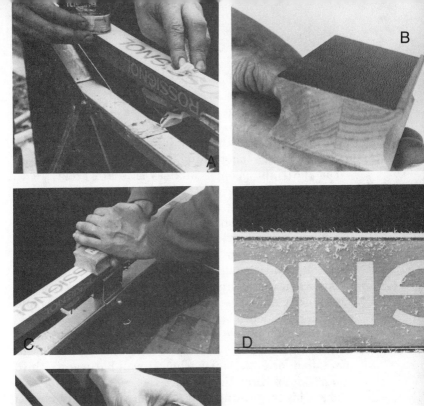

Citizen racers can emulate the elite and turn waxable skis into waxless for difficult snows. Choose a racing ski with a high-quality (extruded) p-Tex base and a fairly stiff hard-powder or klister flex. Clean the base thoroughly with wax remover (A) until it looks like new. Using an abrader (B) — available in ski specialty shops — work from tip toward tail in an area extending from about 10″ in front of the binding to the heel plate (C). Apply a little more force than you would corking out hard wax, except at each end of the pattern, where you want to "feather" it. Working for one to two minutes on each ski will produce an obvious "hairy" base (D). Saturate hairs with silicon preparation (Swix, Holley, Maxiglide) to prevent icing (E). One abrasion may last for one or two dozen outings. You can wax right over it, but if you want to go waxless again, you'll have to begin the whole process again.

Besides the sacrifice of performance to convenience, another trade-off with waxless skis involves effort: while you save waxing time, you usually have to work harder. Waxless skis are usually a bit draggy, so you have to use more effort to push them forward. And you won't get as much free glide — shortening those giddy, free runouts.

For the right people, waxless skis are great. Ned's mother got into cross-country about fifteen years ago when she quit alpine skiing. She found at first that she didn't ski as much as she would have liked to; waxing was a hassle for her. A new pair of waxless skis solved the problem, and now she skis twice as often. We both own waxless skis, and use them for transitional snow or for spring touring in the woods when the klister on the base of waxed skis would turn sludgy and slow from picking up pine needles and other natural debris.

Waxless skis are the logical choice for people who shuffle only a few miles, for occasional skiers who want convenience, and for enthusiasts who ski well but want a third pair of skis for transitional snow. They're good, too, for kids who are just beginning to ski, but be careful not to buy a child's ski that has too long a waxless pattern — if the child isn't heavy enough, the ski won't slide downhill.

And there are geographic considerations. Cold, easy-to-wax-for snow is the exception. A waxable ski may be great for a Vermont vacation, but a waxless ski will allow maximum skiing throughout a New Jersey winter. For those who ski in areas like the Northwest and California, with lots of just-freezing-point weather and rapidly changing snow conditions, waxless skis have become a staple.

When we wrote the first edition of this book four years ago, there were so many waxless skis on the market that picking the best waxless concept was more confusing than picking the wax of the day. Name the geometric design, and manufacturers had tried it. Some skis showed little concern for design: one base had a pattern that looked as if one half of a half dollar had been impressed at regular intervals; another looked as if the company had hired a sedulous slasher to work over the base with a razor blade. The skis were cheap and were often bought by people looking for something just to get around on. Unfortunately, the patterns made it impossible to do that. But the waxless skis now on the market are better—and in models for all skiers, from the mountaineer to the racer.

It's not simply the *kind* of waxless base put on by a manufacturer that makes a difference in performance but also the way in which it is *attached* to the ski and the way in which the design and camber of the ski itself enhances the pattern. For instance, some factories put too much heat and pressure in their ski molds, resulting in a flattening of the pattern and little on-snow grip. Steps, scales, rounds, diamonds, crowns, and smooth bases vary among manufacturers. Mohair has pretty much disappeared as a waxless option. To choose a good waxless ski is tricky; our advice is to try out as many types as you can from rental programs, ski in the typical snow condition of your area, then obtain the help of a good salesperson to make your final decision.

Waxless skis are usually used by folks whose main problem is getting up hills. Choose a ski that has good gripping capability and a soft enough camber so the grip section of the ski will firmly contact the snow. Remember that patterns on the bases of skis make a ski somewhat harder to turn downhill. So don't fail to include some downhill runs in your testing. (A while ago a major ski manufacturer introduced a waxless pattern that resisted even the experts' efforts to turn it right or left.)

Four years ago, Ned fearlessly predicted that "the future will bring great strides forward in waxless skis that are smooth-bottomed and don't wear out, have good glide, turn easily downhill, have base 'patterns' similar to the average size of snow crystals, and can vary somewhat to snow hardness and moisture content—in other words, similar to waxable performance."

"This ski," he said, "is still in the lab." Well, this ski is beginning to appear in the shops. A final report card hasn't been issued, but one thing is becoming clear—the waxless bases must receive occasional attention from steel wool or sandpaper (or even soap and water) for continued effectiveness. Indeed, waxless skis are not maintenance-free. As Swix's Ole Rostad says, "Instead of calling them waxless skis, I prefer to call them 'less-wax skis.'" He means that for best performance (although not essential) the tips and tails of polyethylene-based skis should be prepped

Waxless bases may be smooth or have patterned geometric ridges.

with glider wax to enhance the glide. Some wax companies are offering special spray glider waxes for increased speed of waxless skis in dry and wet snow conditions. Silicone speed spray will help prevent the frustrating tendency of some waxless skis to collect ice in the pattern. In spring conditions, waxless patterns will pick up old klister and crud along the trail, making for a sluggish ski. Liquid wax remover rubbed on with a rag will cure this problem.

One wax company is even planning to market a waxless grip wax to enhance the grip of waxless skis in special snow conditions and as the base pattern wears out. If they're not careful, they'll invent wax all over again!

Length: The old rule of measuring a ski to the wrist of your outstretched arm generally holds true in cross-country. But a six-foot skier may reach up and measure for a two hundred and twenty-centimeter ski. Chances are that two hundred and ten-centimeter would be better, and since it's a more popular size, the likelihood of getting a ski with the proper flex will be increased. A longer ski will be more stable but less maneuverable. Don't go any shorter than ten centimeters from your normal length to try for more maneuverability.

Width: Wider skis are more stable, stronger, and provide more flotation in deep snow but are slower in tracks.

Weight: Lighter means faster in tracks. Heavy skis don't necessarily mean stronger skis. Light equipment allows you to ski with more sensitivity than does heavier gear; when you do something right or wrong, you feel it right away. For long tours and heavy packs you usually need sturdy equipment (although Ned skied 1,250 kilometers in the Arctic on skis forty-seven millimeters wide!). But for track skiing at touring centers, don't overlook the fact that your technique is to a large extent a result of your equipment. You are what you ski on. Those of you who jog know that running with light shoes allows you to go faster, longer, and more easily. A bit of speed over the snow will put cross-country into an entirely different perspective.

Tip flex: To feel this in the shop, simply pull the tip toward you with one hand while feeling the stiffness and transition into the body of the ski with the other hand flat on the ski. Softer tips are faster in machine-set tracks. Stiffer tips are more stable for touring and for holding downhill turns off-track. A longer tip coming farther down into the body of the ski is better for touring and more forgiving since it follows the terrain more easily; shorter tips are better for forceful racing.

Tip splay: Squeeze the skis together. If the tips splay apart down into the body of the skis, they will not track well or turn easily because you are actually skiing on less than the functional part of the ski, guaranteeing a squirrelly ride down any hill.

Torsional stiffness: Twist the ski tip left or right as if you were trying to unscrew the tip from the ski. Stiffer tips give better edge holding for touring, especially on hard-packed snow, while softer tips are better in tracks because they tend not to catch on the sidewalls and ride out of the track.

Camber: Camber is the arch of a ski that distributes your weight over the running surface. When skis are placed bottom to bottom and pressed together, a soft pair will be easy to press together, a stiff pair quite difficult. Each length of ski is given a camber stiffness that is correct for the average weight of a skier who would use that length. For instance, most two hundred and ten-centimeter skis are cambered for 165 to 175 pounds, the average weight of a five-foot-eleven-inch male human. But all pairs within a given length of one brand vary a bit, and brands themselves vary, so if you are light for your height, you should choose a ski with softer camber. Occasionally you must go to a shorter ski to get a softer one.

Racers prefer somewhat more stiffly cambered skis. They're faster because the new pressure distribution patterns keep the base's waxed center section, by and large, up off the snow when the skis are equally weighted, as on downhills and flat stretches of double poling. When the racer kicks and presses down on one ski, the center portion of the base is pressed onto the snow, providing grip. These skis demand an energetic kicking action on well-prepared tracks. (Super-stiff skis are used in klister conditions, softer skis in powder snow.) Stiffer skis also provide positive edge control but demand an expert skier to make them turn.

Softer skis are more forgiving since they are easier to flatten, thus allowing the wax or waxless pattern to bite readily into the snow for uphill grip. They provide better grip for off-track cruising in deep snow and are more easily turned in slow-speed skiing. If we had a choice, we would buy a ski that is a little too soft rather than too stiff. A softer ski may be a little slower, but at least you can make it up the hills with ease.

Sidecut: Many cross-country skis are wider at the tip and tail than at the center. This is called sidecut. You can identify it by placing the sidewalls of the skis together and determining how much space is between skis in the midsection. A light touring ski usually has two to seven millimeters of sidecut, while a touring ski is cut with five to ten millimeters. A ski must have adequate torsional stiffness in the tip to utilize sidecut.

It is assumed that more sidecut (within limits) means the ski will track better and wander less when used in nontrack skiing. Sidecut also helps in holding a turn (bringing you around) and in providing stability at higher speeds. Less sidecut is faster in race tracks (less drag of the flaring tip and tail). It is better in slow pivoting turns because it starts the turn more easily, but it doesn't hold as well during the turn.

Frankly, the verdict on sidecut isn't in. But generally speaking you'll find touring skis with sidecut and racing or light training skis with little or none.

Matched pair: Squeeze the skis together and sight down the closing line. Do they close at the same rate? Is there a hard spot in one? Are they compatible?

Of course no one characteristic makes a ski. Everything must work together to produce a ski which will perform for your intended use and proficiency as a skier. Try to get the skis out on the snow (demo skis from rental programs are your best bet) to find out for yourself. If you've skied on a friend's skis that seem to have the right camber for you, take them along when shopping. Check cambers by pressing together one of the friend's skis and one of those you're considering buying. Form some opinions about your old skis and use them as a basis for evaluating new skis, says a friend of ours who's a racer chaser for a major ski company.

Increasingly, ski shops have ski flex gauges and even electronic testers at their disposal. And ski companies are beginning to denote ski stiffnesses right on the ski. But there's no substitute for having a feel for your skis. A national team skier of 170 pounds might select a ski for powder conditions that took some 135 pounds to flatten. But for a skier of the same weight with a less efficient kick, a softer ski would be in order.

Metal edges: Getting the right camber in a metal-edged ski isn't as much of a problem; it's more a matter of getting any camber at all. Backcountry skis with metal edges and cross-country camber—like a touring ski—have been around for a while. Recently they've been joined by skis with no apparent camber. Squeeze them together and they feel like noodles. What they have is alpine camber. They are designed for maximum turning power.

Which will fit your skiing? If you ask mainly in unbroken snow and want a metal edge for security, go for the backcountry touring ski. It will ski better on the flats. But if your skiing is often lift-served, on steep terrain, or using skins, go for the softer flexing skis—they'll hold much better in turns.

You'll want to demo these skis. A ski that turns well in western powder may not work well on eastern hardpack. A ski designed for fast skiing, including telemark racing, may turn unpredictably for a skier who skis at slower speeds.

Repairs you can do yourself:

• Gouges in bases: Sharp rocks can cause deep scars in the base of polyethylene skis. To repair, dry the base and clean all old wax and grit from the area to be repaired. Trim away any flaps of base material hanging from the wound. Light the end of a P-tex candle and allow it to drip on a fireproof surface until the drippings are soot-free. Hold the candle about a quarter-inch above the base of the ski and fill the scratches. After the patch has cooled and hardened, use a metal scraper to take off the excess. Do final smoothing with fine sandpaper or steel wool.

• Cracks in sidewalls: Use epoxy glue to seal the opening to prevent water seeping into the core. This is not a structural failure.

• Loose binding screws: These can occur if holes are originally drilled too large. Simply plug the holes with steel wool mixed with epoxy, then put the screws back in.

• Delamination: Carefully clean the damaged area and pry open as far as possible. Spread epoxy over the surfaces, pushing it as far into the delamination as possible. Squeeze out surplus epoxy, wrap with wax paper, and place wood or metal splints on either side of the ski to act as a form for even pressure. Clamp snugly with C clamps, being careful not to press all the glue out.

Summer storage: Give your skis a thick coat of glider wax on the full length of the base and leave it unscraped. Then just set them against the wall in a relatively cool, dry room.

Rock skis: Failure to make these repairs—or the regular need to make them—means that you may have a pair of "rock skis" at hand. Value them! They will let you ski early in the season or through a poor snow year. At such times, if you ski on a snowed-over dirt road, you'll likely hear an emphatic click as you graze an emerging rock, or the sickening grate of ski on gravel as a turn pushes snow aside. In such scratchy conditions, rock skis are vital. The shabbiest, most expendable pair of skis may become the most valued. How shabby? Well, about like those of our friend Stewart Ruth. The tops of his skis are checkered and pitted from wayward pole plants. The sidewalls are gouged deeply enough to allow an intimate look at the skis' interior, the base on one ski has lifted away from the tail and flaps

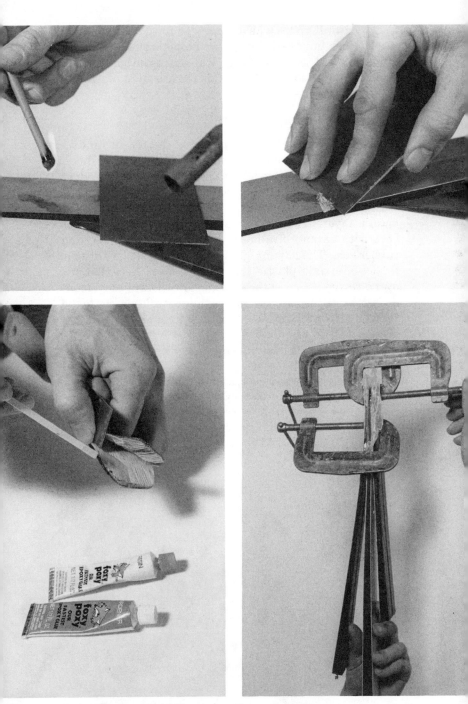

Repairing skis: *(Top)* Fill and smooth gouges in bases.
(Bottom) Glue and splint delaminations.

freely. Several grooves have appeared in the bottom, joining the one put there by the manufacturer. There is an almost total absence of camber, which is, as he points out, a real advantage as early season tracks are often indefinite, calling for a soft ski.

Boots and Bindings

In 1979 we wrote that, considering the recent innovations in downhill boots and bindings and in running shoes, similar advances would follow in cross-country. Indeed, at that time they had already begun, as plastic-soled boots with fifty-millimeter or thirty-eight-millimeter mounts became favored by racers over the long-established leather boot with seventy-five-millimeter Donald Duck toe and rubber sole. The advantages are considerable. With their torsionally rigid plastic soles and grooved heel that fits over a wedge nailed to the ski, the new boots offer tremendous downhill control. And since the boot sole clamps to the ski well in front of the toes, heel lift is freer and there is less pressure on instep and toes.

Further innovations came quickly, with design changes

Boots for track skiing and racing share common features (A), especially a wedge and groove underfoot for better downhill control (B, C, D). In one design (E), the ski itself becomes the wedge as sides of boot sole overlap it.

A

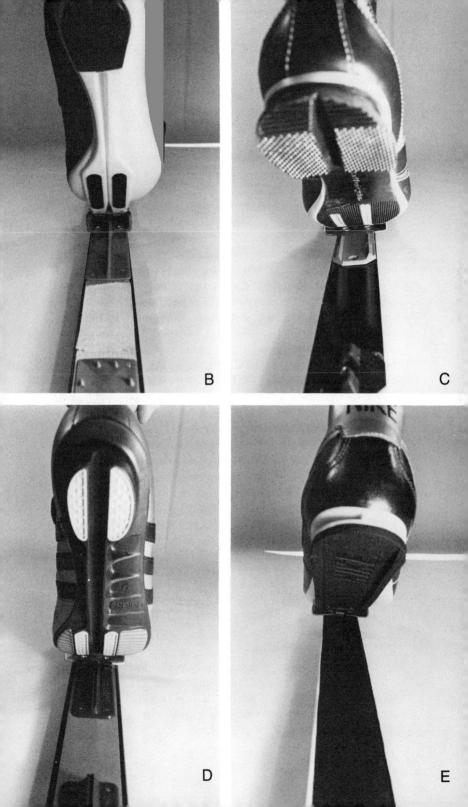

B

C

D

E

in boots and bindings more dramatic than in skis. Often one company's boot is compatible only with that company's bindings; now we're talking "systems." What many have in common is that they extend the wedge and groove concept to the ball of the foot area or even along the whole length of the sole. This yields some real advantages, like better control in the herringbone and skate and better downhill control. Alpine skiers find they can ski more with their knees, as they're accustomed to in plastic alpine boots. Beginning skiers, we've found, will be able to redistribute pressure along their foot, thus taking pressure off their hips in long, defensive snowplows. Faced with an array of boot-binding systems, beginning skiers often wonder "is this stuff just for racers?" Emphatically not. These systems offer more control to everyone. An experienced skier whose seventy-five-millimeter boots have worn out should consider them.

Which to choose? First, the one that fits best, snug in the heel but with some room in the toes—like your favorite running or tennis shoes. But don't just walk around a store in them. Clip into a binding mounted on a "demo" board available in most stores to check for flex and fit. Best of all, take the boot and binding out for a ski, if possible.

If the boot doesn't fit quite right, don't make the beginner's mistake of cramming in extra socks to take up extra room. Instead resort to insoles (sockliners, foot beds— plenty of loose terminology here). Following the lead of running shoes, many of the new ski boots have foam insoles. Don't hesitate to take them out and substitute thicker or thinner ones; some stores now carry almost as many kinds of insoles as they do boots. No matter what kind you choose, remove them after skiing for quicker boot drying.

Does all this mean that the seventy-five-millimeter rubber-soled boot is dead? For touring at ski centers and parks, they're on the way out. But there are some problems with the new rigs. The plastic soles are slippery: not meant for driving, walking, and especially rock scrambling. And some of the boot-binding attachments load up in deep snow, inhibiting control. So if your style is off track, break-your-own-trail in the deep stuff, a higher-cut seventy-five-millimeter boot is still a good choice.

Poles

Poles are often overlooked, but they are a functional part of your skiing. Many beginners feel awkward with their poles because they've gotten them too long or too short or with straps that can't be properly adjusted. The right pole will help you ski better and provide a good percentage of your power instead of merely the balance of outriggers.

The proper pole means the proper basket. Years ago, you had your choice of round, round, or round. Great for touring, especially in unpacked snow, but in a hard track the front half of the basket tended to lever the pole out of the snow. The newer, asymmetric half-baskets allow stronger, more forceful poling. But try to use them for downhill checking or support for a kick turn on steep slopes and you'll find them skittering over the snow instead of sticking in. Still, if you're a park and touring center skier, an exercise skier or racer, these are the way to go. Shafts can be fiberglass, aluminum, or more exotic, super-light fibers. The stiffer the shaft, the better—poling energy will be transmitted directly to the snow. One thing hasn't changed much: the pole should fit snugly in your armpit as you stand upright. Better to go slightly shorter if you have to.

For backcountry, we like high-quality aluminum poles whose shafts are threaded at the top. Buy them in an alpine length (some fifteen–twenty centimeters shorter

Poles. Round baskets for mountaineering, but even touring baskets have acquired more elliptical shapes, influenced by the half-baskets on racing poles.

than normal), which will be perfect for steep descents. Pull off the grip, screw on an extension, and you have the proper length for poling in and out of the high country.

Backcountry Equipment . . . and Excess

But backcountry skiing doesn't necessarily mean tele-mark skiing and the gear that has evolved for it in the last four years. While very high-cut and rigid seventy-five-millimeter boots will be the choice of the skier who regu-larly opts for steep, mountainous terrain or snows that can be changeable and dangerous and for the lift-riding tele-marker, you don't need that much weight for less intense off-track cruising. For that matter, you can forgo the metal-edged skis, which some skiers believe are part of the package, and choose instead a wide ski whose edgeless light weight will allow some backcountry kick-and-glide. One of our friends, high-booted and metal-edged, calls his forward progress toward a peak "hiking," not skiing. And on heavy gear, with ski skins, it can be a slow slog. Neither this skier nor his fellow guides use any of the several devices on the market that allow free heel lift for striding but lock heels down laterally. These don't do much for an insubstantial boot, and we feel they increase the risk of serious injury, especially when skiing with a pack in heavy snows.

Backpacks

Skiing with a pack is never as pleasant as skiing free, but for all-day tours it is necessary to bring along extra clothing, waxes, map, sunglasses, and a few things to eat; as well as a spare tip in case of a broken ski, space blanket, and matches for emergencies. Include tape—adhesive tape for blisters and fiberglass strapping tape for repairing broken equipment. Tape is an instant all-inclusive repair kit. (People have even been known to tape bindings back onto skis or a broken or delaminated boot right to the ski!)

A good-sized fanny pack may well be all you need for fast tours close to home, since it hinders skiing movement very little. But for ventures farther afield, you'll want a bit more capacity. We prefer a day pack that is fairly tall but not too wide, so arms can swing freely. We've found that most climbing rucksacks are a pretty good bet: they'll provide

Backpacks are a necessity for extended treks. Sleds are practical for transporting heavy loads of gear for expeditions.

enough capacity so you don't have to cram everything in so tightly that you end up with a tight "ball" on your back, which is uncomfortable.

The problem on multiday treks of course is how to carry all the gear and still enjoy the experience. The first step is to choose a large pack that is comfortable, stable, and simply designed. Most designers get carried away with the process of designing and forget that serious backpackers want only what is necessary out on the trail. Remember that you'll be operating cords and buckles on the trail with cold hands or mittens. Intricate systems often let you down when you most need them. For control while touring, stay away from packs that roll with every skiing movement. Choose one of the specially designed soft packs or interior-frame packs which "cling" to your body. This is especially critical in downhill skiing situations where a loose pack will exaggerate any error you commit, often throwing you off balance and leading to bruising or dangerous falls. The totally soft packs are more stable but more difficult to pack. The manner in which they are packed forms the frame. Be careful not to have hard objects jabbing into your back.

We like soft packs best for medium-weight loads. For heavy and larger loads on extensive tours, go with an interior-frame pack which helps distribute the load more comfortably. Important for ease of carrying loads is a sophisticated yet simple arrangement by which an auxiliary strap "picks" the weight up off your shoulder straps, thereby lessening the pressure on your shoulders, especially while poling. (The trade-off here is that the pack tends to sway a bit more.) A sternum strap which links the two shoulder straps across the chest further frees shoulder movement and eliminates sway. Make sure all straps can be adjusted while you are skiing. A wide waist belt which is padded at the hips and easily closed by Velcro or quick-release buckle further fastens the pack so it almost becomes part of your body and moves with it.

Make sure that pockets are removable so you can use the pack for faster skiing and complete poling extension if you wish. Side straps which can be used to carry skis on your pack are useful in case you have to walk the last couple of miles of the tour. Compartmentalize your gear by packing certain similar things in nylon stuff sacks and labeling each. In this way you'll maintain some order when unpacking at your campsite. Pack heavy items low and closest to your back for maximum stability. Items needed during the day should be placed on top for easy access.

As you might suspect, to ski with a heavy backpack you'll have to make considerable adjustments in your technique. Ned recalls starting off around Mount McKinley with eighty pounds on his back (his skis were only forty-seven-millimeters wide and he used three-pin bindings). At first he could barely support the load, to say nothing of moving forward or negotiating downhills.

Weight on your back accentuates any mistake, so the key is not to make any mistakes. Ski very conservatively with a heavy pack, often electing to make a series of traverses down a slope rather than link turns. Unless you require additional pushing power uphill, use your poles relatively little in comparison to skiing without a pack and keep your hands low as if you're walking. Since packs press down on the muscles running across the top of the shoulders, raising the hands high in front brings fatigue faster. Falling with the persuasion of a big pack is never subtle. Try your utmost to maintain your balance, but when all is obviously lost, let go and relax, trying to avoid jamming head and shoulders into hard snow or rocks. Ned's McKinley trip very nearly had to be aborted after Allan Bard dislocated a shoulder in a fall that was vicious only because of the weight he carried.

Sleds

During Ned's High Arctic Expedition to Ellesmere Island each man hauled his gear in an eight-foot fiberglass sled. It was the only practical means of transporting 240 pounds apiece. They got the sleds through chaotic ocean pack ice, up steep glacier tongues, and down rocky river valleys. Of course you must choose your route carefully — certain terrain eliminates sled hauling — but consider a sled as a practical alternative to humping heavy backpacks. We prefer boat-type sleds which float on the snow and have angled sides to prevent capsizing in deep snow. Long sleds tend to even out small terrain variations. Rigid fiberglass pulling poles control the sled effectively; some come equipped with springs at the junction to the waist belt for easier striding action. We prefer a chest-shoulder-and-waist-combination pulling harness.

Other uses for sleds are for toting the small kids on a tour or packing supplies into a hunting or fishing camp or off-the-road homestead.

Waxing

Waxing may be a little more complicated than making a peanut butter and jelly sandwich, but the aim is to keep it simple. You can pretty much do what you want, imitating the racer's iridescent combination of klisters or making use of a less flamboyant two-wax system for touring. We've seen it all on the waxing benches at ski touring centers, where "the wax of the day" is often pursued with near frenzy, yielding results that would satisfy an abstract expressionist.

Why take the time and trouble to wax well? You'll have "fast" skis that not only grip well but glide easily. Many beginning and even intermediate skiers are fearful of speed. "I don't want a fast ski," they protest. But if they think of it as doing less work, their response will be quite different.

How Wax Works

Watching good cross-country skiers, you might believe that one wax will allow a person to ski on the flat, uphill, and down with only a slight change in technique.

How is this possible? We turn to ski scientist Mike Brady, who has long been on intimate terms with ski waxes and ski bottoms: "A waxed ski behaves this way because small microscopic irregularities of the snow surface penetrate the wax just enough to allow a good grip when a ski is weighted, yet allow a moving ski to glide." If you use wax that is too soft, the snow particles will penetrate too far into the wax and you'll be able to walk up the side of a barn door, but you'll be so sticky that you'll have to walk down the other side as well. If you put wax on that is too hard, the snow particles cannot penetrate at all. Your skis will perform like an alpine ski. They'll be like greased lightning on the downhills but in definite need of a mechanical lift on the uphills.

A day's skiing may require waxing changes.

Grip Waxes

These waxes give you purchase on the snow. (Glide waxes, to be covered later, provide faster glide.) Grip waxes can be divided into three categories. Hard wax is for snow that is in its original condition. It may have been on the ground for several days, but it still hasn't melted, refrozen, or otherwise changed. Klister is tacky fluid, the consistency of toothpaste, for snow that has melted once, melted and refrozen, or melted, refrozen, and melted several times. After all these changes the original prickly crystals have become so rounded off that they can't penetrate hard wax; hence oozy klister.

Klister-wax is halfway between hard wax and klister for use at temperatures around freezing. It's messy stuff and fortunately seldom used.

Ingredients: All waxes, both hard and klisters, share some common ingredients, although in different proportions depending on the type of snow for which they are intended (big wax firms no longer use beeswax, alas for the romantic legends of the past):

• Petroleum wax for water repellency.

• Synthetic rubber for adhesion.

• Oil and vaseline to soften hard wax; synthetic resin to soften klister.

Ned had the curious experience of touring the catacombs of the Swix wax factory in Norway. There, in huge vats, are gallons and gallons of wax, bubbling and steaming and ready to be piped up to the cannister-filling machines. Despite a commonly held belief of skiers flummoxed by waxing, there was no eye of newt, toe of frog, wool of bat, or tongue of dog among the ingredients.

Selection: The cannisters and tubes which receive the molten wax are color-coded for easy selection. It pretty much follows the spectrum: colder colors for cold snow — green and blue; warmer colors for warmer snow — purple, red, and yellow. Since we first wrote this book, hard waxes and klisters have proliferated. No cause for anxiety. The simple fact is that the more waxes you have available, the more likely you'll have one just right for the snow conditions on a particular day. Generally, companies have added harder and softer waxes on each side of the waxes in the basic colors. You'll probably find that these waxes grip or glide better than the basics, so that touring skiers now are more comfortable with the harder and softer versions of, say, red wax, than to that venerable wax itself. Indeed, the harder red and softer blue are so useful, they're virtually basic. Klisters have gotten the same treatment. The fine tuning here may be a bit much for touring skiers and best left to racers. But not to be neglected is the new universal klister, which nearly lives up to its name, and the klisters for very wet snow — just right for spring skiing.

When touring center instructors put a waxing suggestion on the blackboard, they haven't had to sacrifice a sheep or turn to a computer to get the wax of the day. They've simply checked the temperature on a thermometer located in the shade and determined whether the snow has been melted and refrozen (turning it into klister snow) and matched that with the directions on a cannister of wax. After a while you'll find that it becomes fairly routine: if the temperature is in the low twenties, red wax won't get a second glance. But humidity can make a difference. A humid day with temperatures in the twenties (Fahrenheit) might have you reaching for purple wax instead of the more obvious blue.

Many people take the posted "wax of the day" as an article of faith. One instructor friend of ours answered a telephone inquiry by saying, "Right now we're using special green." Several seconds passed, then a desperate and incredulous voice on the other end asked, "You mean it might change?" Change it may, and if you want to ski successfully you'll have to be willing to make some changes in your wax. With the wide changes of temperature in the Sierra, some days will call for a complete ransacking of the wax box; yet Alaskan skiers may cruise serenely on special green for days on end. Skiers leaving a touring center for a higher ridge may find that as the snow gets colder the higher they go, the purple wax that worked well for the first couple of kilometers has to be scraped off and replaced with blue.

Application: Most skiers, even beginners, won't have an especially hard time figuring out what wax to use. Problems occur putting the wax on the ski bottom. (One inquiring skier we overheard complaining about slippery skis was told to add a little more purple underfoot. He sat down straightaway and waxed his shoes.) Although blue may be the right wax, it will be awfully slow if applied like stucco; likewise red klister if applied thickly enough to merit anchovies and mushrooms. If it doubt, ask. Many touring center operators bewail skiers' resistance to waxing assistance cheerfully offered. "If I put on a waxing clinic," says one of our friends, "it's a zero draw. But if I simply start waxing a ski in full view, I draw a crowd."

Hard wax is easy as long as your ski is dry (outside you may have to wipe the moisture off with a gloved hand or

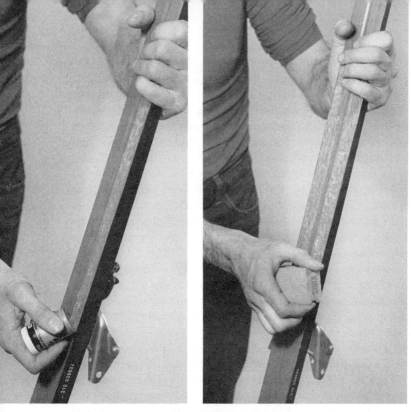

Crayon hard wax on, then cork smooth.

bandana). Peel back the wax tin and simply rub it on as if you were coloring the base with a crayon. Using the edge of the wax results in a smoother layer. Rub the wax out with short vigorous strokes of a cork (preferably a synthetic one) to make it faster and more durable. If you run your thumbnail over your ski bottom and don't roll up much wax, you haven't put enough on.

Klister is rowdy stuff and will readily transfer itself to your hands, clothes, and hair if not kept on a short leash. Warm the tube slightly with a torch, near a fire, or in your hand to make it squeezable (you don't have to bring it to a rolling boil); cold klister is impossible to extract from the tube. Squeeze a thin ribbon down each side of the groove by pressing the nozzle flat against the ski bottom. Smooth it out with the plastic spatula provided with most klisters. Or use your palm — handcleaner to follow. If you wax outside, you need a torch for spreading. If it runs over the side of the ski, you've put too much on; mop up the excess with a rag. If you're mixing klisters, dab alternate horizontal strips on each side of the groove, for an overall chevron pattern. A couple of inches between each dab should be sufficient. Apply a little heat and mix. Experienced skiers know that silver klisters give great grip on transitional snows and that they help keep other mixed-in klisters free of debris in spring snow. Again, be very sparing in putting it on and mixing it in.

Klister wax comes in a can like hard wax but behaves like klister. Daub it on in distinct intervals of a couple of inches and be prepared for the festoons of wax attaching cannister to ski bottoms even at arm's length—a bubble gum riot. Less is more here; as a matter of fact less may still be too much. Smooth it out with a torch and rag or a cork used for this wax only. Where to put it? The middle of your ski is your waxing target, from the heel plate forward. How far forward? Two feet may be enough. But if you're skiing in tracks that are soft and filling in with new snow, wax almost to the beginning of the tip.

Two-wax systems: If you're just getting started in skiing or don't want to face the array of waxes and klisters (or are color blind), you can ski very nicely using the two-wax systems now on the market. They're so reliable Ned has used them on long multiweek ski expeditions. They're

Squeeze klister on, then spread evenly.

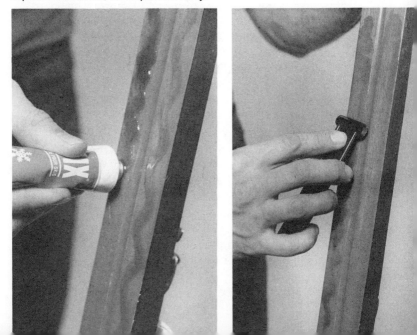

simple to use: one wax for dry and powdery snow below freezing and one wax for wet and packing snow above. In the Swix system, "gold wax is for cold, silver is for slop." In others, it's above and below freezing. The waxes are formulated to respond to a wide range of moisture and hardness in the snow: so even with only two waxes you get adequate performance. The secret is a subtle application of layers. Apply them thinly and cork them in well for cold dry snow. Be sparing in your first application, and if the skis are still slipping as the day warms, continue to add more wax. You get more grip not by switching to a different wax but by adding a thicker, rougher, longer coat. When the conditions get really slushy, you may have to apply up to a half cannister of wet wax to get adequate grip.

A paper-thin layer of cold-snow wax, polished well with a waxing cork, works like hard green wax. A long, thick, unpolished layer of the same wax works like hard purple. A thin layer of wet-snow wax works like hard red, while a thick layer works about like red klister, but only on the flat. If you need real climbing grip in old slushy snow, you'd better use some regular red klister.

Because two-wax systems are very forgiving as snow hardness changes radically at the freezing point (the ultimately frustrating waxing temperature) and tend not to ice up as readily as regular wax, they work excellently in snow just at the freezing point and in snow lying on unfrozen ground, which is common in cities and southern areas. You can ski around Central Park in New York City, then head to Vermont or Colorado and use the same waxing system—it's adaptable. In difficult waxing conditions, even racers use it. After you become comfortable with the two-wax system you might want to try a little finer tuning by moving into the full waxing spectrum.

Wax removal and ski purification: Remove as much wax as possible with a scraper, working from tail to tip so that you roll up a ball of wax. If you're out on the trail, this is as much cleaning as you'll have to do. Otherwise, to prevent buildup of old waxes, scrape and then use a solvent or commercial wax remover with a rag. You can also use a torch to melt the wax and wipe it away, but be cautious and keep the torch moving so you don't melt the base of the ski. Solvents are a much safer bet.

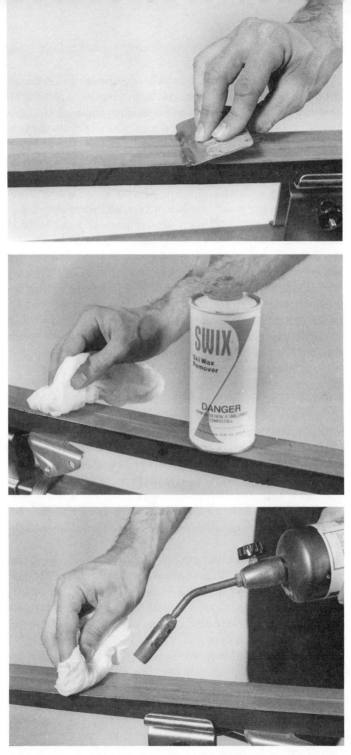

Scrape off old wax, then wipe clean with a rag and solvent or torch.

Troubleshooting: If your skis are slippery and do not climb, your wax is too hard, you didn't put enough of it on, or what you put on has worn off. Before you make adjustments, make sure you've skied a couple hundred yards so the wax gets cooled off and skied in. (Skis should be set outside after waxing and allowed to cool off.) Begin by adding a longer kicker of the same wax, especially in soft tracks filling in with snow or bushwhacking in deep snow. Then go to a light application of the next warmer wax.

If your skis do not glide, you may have put on too much wax or too soft a wax, sometimes creating an instant six-inch platform of snow underfoot. Scrape and go to a colder wax.

Problems with klister usually come from putting too much on, causing it to ice up, resulting in skis that are both slow in gliding (ice in the klister) and slippery (layer of ice particles trying to penetrate iced-up klister). Four years ago, we suggested that touring skiers wax for the dryest snow to be encountered. Better, we said, to slip in the sunny meadow than stick in the shady forest.

Since then, there have been a couple of winters in our haunts whose prevailing conditions have called for more sophisticated waxing if skiing is to be had. And so the wax of the day has been posted as, say, "purple klister covered by purple hard wax." And virtually no one panicked! There were some questions, of course, especially from those who had been told that it's softer wax over hard, jelly over peanut butter. But for granular snow near the touring center and drier snow higher up, this combination was the best call.

How to do it? Put on a thin layer of klister and set the skis outside to freeze it. Then delicately smooth on some hard wax after softening it in the flame of a torch. Cork lightly. So, too, for hard waxes. In our area, successful waxing for early-season powder can mean a "cushion" of special red covered with extra blue.

To prevent wax from wearing off, there are a couple of solutions. The simplest is to heat the first layer into the ski base with a torch or iron, smoothing it out with a rag, to create a good bond. Set the skis outside to cool, then cork the next layer in.

If the snow is icy and abrasive, take the time to use

klister wax's even stickier cousin, binder wax. Dab it on cautiously or freeze it outside and you'll be able to crayon it on. Smooth it out thinly with a warm iron or torch and cork; then apply a layer of hard wax, mixing it in with an iron. Set the skis outside and carefully cork in an additional layer or two of hard wax. It can't be denied that this is a little tedious. Get some help the first time. But it's worth the trouble because you will get better climb uphill and not have to stop in mid-tour to rewax. Becoming adept with binder is more important than ever, since many parks and touring centers now have sophisticated trail-grooming machinery that can render ice or crust into a very skiable—but very abrasive—granular snow. It's either binder or continued rewaxing, as downhills scour wax from your skis.

Purple and red hard waxes can get pretty gummy if crayoned on warm. Instead stroke them on gently in one direction when the wax is cold.

If you still have plenty of wax on at the end of the day's tour and snow conditions will be the same the next day, go with your old wax.

Beginners usually complain about slippery skis; for them a longer kicker of grip wax is a good idea. More expert skiers wail about slow skis; they'll want to experiment with the length, position, and thickness of the kicker and even get to know the different characteristics of the same color wax in different brands. The best way to experiment is to wax each ski differently; you can always adjust the less adequate ski out on the trail.

Wax in anticipation for the day's conditions—especially true for spring skiing. If it's twenty degrees early in the morning but will warm up to fifty at noon, calling for red klister, put the red on early instead of working up through blue and purple. Otherwise you're letting yourself in for a Hieronymous Bosch klister klassic.

A good wax job is worth the effort. Students who have switched skis with their instructors are usually astonished at how smoothly they glide and how little effort is needed to ski on them.

Zero degree frustration: When snow falls at the freezing point, it occasions what is known as a "wax day." Which is not to say just that you'll use wax, but that you may use fourteen or so in various combinations. Frustration is the order of the day and madness not far off. People are not amused by an instructor who throws up his hands and says, "I don't know," to a question about the wax most suitable for this sleazy, incorrigible, wayward, coy, devilish snow.

Why? As the temperature approaches freezing, the snow decreases in hardness. Because there is less snow crystal penetration, you need a softer wax. At and around freezing, the rate of change of snow crystal hardness is so accelerated that for every tenth of a degree of temperature change, the snow hardness changes manyfold. Since no wax composition can keep up with this rate of change of snow hardness, you need many different waxes for small changes in temperature (and a lot of patience).

Glide Waxes

You can ski quite well without paying attention to either the tips or tails of your skis, but even better if you take the time to pamper them with a little wax, thus adding performance and durability to the skis. This is vital for racing skis, but also important for touring skis, because an increasing number of them have polyethylene bases similar to those on the racing skis.

There is no doubt that glide wax adds tremendously to your speed, especially in wet snow conditions. This is particularly true in stiff racing skis which ride only on the glide wax of tips and tails when going downhill. The special design of racing skis actually keeps the center gripping section up off the snow to reduce drag and increase speed.

Although you can use the same glide wax that alpine skiers use, it can get pretty complicated. It's a lot easier to use the special cross-country gliders color-coded to the gripping wax. Mercifully, there are a lot fewer of them — no specials, extras, and supers. And touring skiers can simplify even further. Use one wax for conditions above freezing and another for those below. As it turns out, one wax in a company's line may have an especially wide range. Rex's blue glider, for example, has a much wider range than their purple. But Swix's purple glider is their all-purpose lubrication. The length of your glider zone is

Glide waxing is vital for racing.

determined by the length of your kicking zone; hot wax only where you're not going to place your kicker wax. (Glide wax must be applied with heat if it is to bond with the polyethylene base.)

Just as you wax the middle of the ski according to the snow conditions for grip, so do you vary the glide wax on tips and tails for maximum glide. Racers and fast recreational skiers may change their glide wax daily; other skiers will not appreciate the performance difference enough to warrant the extra preparation time. They'll rewax only when they see whitish streaks on tips and tails.

How to put on glide wax: Place the skis on a level bench with the bases up. Heat a waxing iron with a torch or, better, use an electric iron set at "wool." Choose the appropriate glider wax or equivalent alpine wax. Press the wax against the iron, dripping a line along each side of the groove, leaving the center sixty to eighty centimeters unwaxed to aid adhesion of the running grip wax which will be put there. Avoid heating the wax so much that it smokes.

Smooth out the wax by running the iron back and forth over the base. Keep the iron moving or you'll melt the plastic or cause a delamination. Reach under the ski and feel the top skin. When it's warm, you've ironed enough. Allow the wax to cool.

Scrape excess wax off the base with a plastic scraper that will not damage the bottom. Don't forget to remove excess wax from the groove with a rounded plastic item like the head of a klister spreader and to clean up drippings on the sidewall. The final result should be a smooth base from which all wax seems to have been removed.

One further step will help skis glide better in wet snow and spring conditions, when suction between water in the snow and your ski makes you feel you're kicking hard but getting little glide. When you scrape off the glider wax do it gently, leaving on a thicker coat than you would for colder snow. Then striate the wax by taking several firm strokes with a wire brush, working from tip toward tail.

Base prepping: Some skis come off the rack with a rough and slightly hairy plastic base, although more manufacturers are microplaning the bases smooth at the factory. To smooth out the base, hot wax as outlined above but scrape with a metal scraper to take off hairs along with excess wax, then hot wax again, scraping with a plastic scraper.

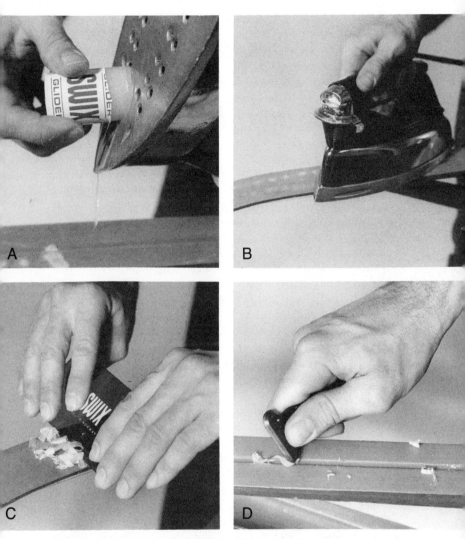

Glide waxing. Drip melted wax onto ski base (A). If you lack a
steady hand, hold tip of iron against base. Iron wax in, a couple of
minutes on tips and tails (B). Scrape with plastic scraper (C).
Remove wax from groove (D).

Cross-country for Kids

Cross-country is a great family sport—available, affordable, and full of shared experiences and challenges, like making it to the top of the ridge for a picnic and the annual family snowball fight followed by the cannon ball derby on the descent. Still, over the years, we've heard parents admit that the sport that's billed as fun for the family can be anything but. You have to tailor the touring to the child, looking at the sport from the child's view.

Accordingly, we thought we'd better get some children's opinions on cross-country. We asked the Hamilton sisters, Dana and Nina, of Moscow, Vermont. In the first edition of this book, when they were nine and six, respectively, they contributed opinions on how kids should dress for cross-country. Four years later and now accomplished skiers of both alpine and cross-country persuasions, they were willing to make some suggestions on how to get kids going.

Start kids out on easy terrain with flats, bumps, little hills, and tracks for easy sliding and striding. Dana and Nina agree. "Go up a long hill? You wouldn't do that the first day," said Nina. "If you do too much, it's not fun." Above all don't teach too much; let them discover skiing for themselves, relying on their considerable abilities as imitators. Use plenty of games—almost anything that works on grass will work on snow: redlight-greenlight, tag, soccer, hockey, foxes and hares, relay races, follow the leader. And what works for American children works as well for Chinese children, some of whom skied on skis made of single pieces of walnut, as Ned Gillette and Jan Reynolds discovered in 1980 as guest instructors in northeastern China. When it came to teaching *huaxue* (skiing), games solved every language problem.

Not only do children have a short attention span, but they get tired as well. So give them a break and have some

Games will help keep it fun.

fun yourself by giving them a ride, towing your little ones uphill or along the trail by having them hold onto your extended ski pole. They'll quickly get a sense of riding a gliding ski, of what happens when they lean forward or back. Older children can make a chain of ski poles, looping straps around baskets. Space them out so they won't ski over each other, and tow the whole bunch. Or put a child between your legs, holding onto your knees, with the little skis in the track and the big ones outside as you double-pole. Many kids like a good push at the end so they can do some free sliding.

Don't get technical. Skiing is a natural activity for children, and it's pretty likely that they aren't concerned with a lot of the hangups that adults are, like falling over, or the proper rhythm for making turns downhill (chances are it's more thrilling to bomb the slope straight, anyway). The

Top to bottom: Simon says, "Bob up and down." Sneaking along.
Lending a hand with the pole pull.

two skiers in the middle photograph are skiing well for five-year-olds — or any age, for that matter. They haven't been told to get their weight out onto the forward ski but instead are doing some sneaking, creeping up on a larger skier. Don't worry if your kids end up doing something besides what you had intended. As long as they're out in the snow, they're learning and discovering things for themselves. Be available to lend encouragement, but don't hover about in a heavy-handed way.

One way to make sure that parents don't push their children too hard, say the Hamilton sisters, is to take a child's friend along—"it's more fun to ski with a friend," says Dana. Still, Nina notes the importance of having parents along as proven procurers of hot chocolate after an outing.

Children will discover downhills on their own and will relish falling a good deal more than you do. All you may need to do is help extract one of them from a snowbank and provide an occasional lift back up the hill, but a bit of instruction on how to get up after a fall will produce real confidence to try new things. Squatting on their skis as they move downhill will keep kids close to the snow and secure. They can push off and do some paddling with their hands, and then, in a Simon Says fashion, bob up and down until they're finally comfortable on their skis.

With very small people or ones that are not having much fun on downhills, you might try holding the child in front of you, his skis running straight as yours snowplow in a wide wedge. This way the child will glide securely and you can keep him in balance, letting go for longer periods as confidence builds. Kids won't respond very well to a lecture on how to turn, but set up a slalom course with ski poles if slalom poles aren't handy, start to snake down yourself, and watch them turn as they begin to follow you. Limbo events and a natural or constructed jump are real attractions for the close-to-the-snow crowd.

If your child is a preschooler, he or she still may be ready for skiing—three years old may not be too early for sliding and tumbling. If it seems to be, how about a trip on a ski-pulled sled? Remember that for little kids, skiing is merely a part of winter's pleasures. Our associate Andrew Jaspersohn, a sturdy three-year-old, likes to do some slid-

"Armpit aid" turns initial security into self-sufficiency.

Slalom courses teach coordination.

ing, sans poles, in a well-set track. But he also likes to take off his skis and jump off the trail and roll down a hill to achieve Oneness with the snow. And he can get quite involved with setting bun to snowbank at his local touring center. All part of the cross-country experience.

You don't need much of an outlay in either clothes or equipment to get kids started. Snowpants and sweaters and a jacket or vest should do it, say the Hamiltons, who suggest taking extra mittens or gloves along. You don't need to bundle kids up until movement is nearly impossible, but you should dress them with anticipation of plenty of time rolling in the deep stuff whether in cold Vermont or soggy Oregon. Waxless skis are great for kids, or, if you use waxable skis, make sure they are well waxed to ensure enjoyment. Shorter rather than longer skis make playing and maneuvering second nature. For really little ones a simple strap binding that can be worn with their own winter boots is all you need. For these younger, shorter skiers, poles will only be an encumbrance. Don't worry about older kids outgrowing skis, boots, and poles—there always seems to be a market for second-hand equipment, and many communities have a ski swap in the fall. But you can get extra life out of ski boots by fitting them with an insole to begin with, taking it out when feet grow.

As kids get a bit older, encourage them to enter a few races. Not only can this be fun if approached in the right way, but a bit of competitive peer pressure will often supply the interest and challenge necessary for kids to want to stay with this outdoor sport.

Low key racing for the fun of it.

The Flying Tip Grab.

Silly Skiing

"This ain't no Oslo,
This ain't no Putney.
This ain't but foolin' around."
(with apologies to the Talking Heads)

Ned Gillette, John Dostal, and two other adult males come shooting out of the trees, off a trail, and onto a meadow. They are, of course, on their skis. And more. Still attached to their bindings, they are also on their knees and elbows, pulling ski tips back for speed. They slide to a stop near an elderly skier. She looks down and, over the giggling going on below, says "Tough wax day, boys?"

Indeed it had been. And a leaden day at the end of a long season. Time for some fun, time for the just-completed Flying Tip Grab. Which had followed a few Bullies in the telemark position. In a tribute to Bullwinkle Moose, pole handles were elevated to ear level, shafts angling out at the proper forty-five degrees.

Silly? Absolutely. Fun? Assuredly.

Tandem skiing.

On or off skis, we'll have our jest. And you might want to as well. To the aforementioned maneuvers, you might want to add some tandem skiing. And every now and then, throw in a Putney road crossing to keep your associates on their toes.

John Dostal (left) and Ned Gillette.

About the authors:

Ned Gillette and John Dostal can make a strong claim to be North America's experts on all aspects of cross-country skiing, serving as advisors to the ski industry. Gillette is a veteran of the U.S. Olympics ski team, former director of Nordic and Alpine ski schools in Vermont, Colorado, and California, pioneer of adventure skiing in China, Tibet, Nepal, Pakistan, New Zealand, Alaska, and the high Arctic. Dostal is director of skiing at Vermont's Trapp Family Lodge, one of America's foremost cross-country ski centers, and an editor of Ski Magazine's Cross Country and Ski Business. Both authors have contributed a wide range of articles on skiing to national magazines.

Index